The
Cognitive
Behavioral Therapy
WORKBOOK
FOR
LEADERS

HOW IMPROVING YOUR MENTAL HEALTH IS ESSENTIAL TO AVOIDING BURNOUT AND LEADING MORE EFFECTIVELY

JULIAN BARLING, PHD
SIMON A. REGO, PSYD

New Harbinger Publications, Inc.

Publisher's Note

NEW HARBINGER PUBLICATIONS is a registered trademark of New Harbinger Publications, Inc.

New Harbinger Publications is an employee-owned company.

Copyright © 2026 by Julian Barling and Simon A. Rego
New Harbinger Publications, Inc.
5720 Shattuck Avenue
Oakland, CA 94609
www.newharbinger.com

All Rights Reserved

Cover design by Sara Christian

Acquired by Ryan Buresh

Edited by Jody Bower

Library of Congress Cataloging-in-Publication Data on file

Printed in the United States of America

28   27   26

10   9   8   7   6   5   4   3   2   1

First Printing

To my amazing wife and children, Janice, Seth, Monique, Steve, and Stephanie:
Your dedication to making the world a better place fills me with pride and purpose.

To my cherished grandchildren, Miles, Felix, Milena, and Mady:
You bring endless joy and light into my life.

—Julian

To my brilliant wife, Adriana E. Rego, MD,
medical director of the Columbia University Clinic for Anxiety and
Related Disorders (CUCARD) in New York City and Westchester:
Your compassion, commitment to clinical excellence, and unwavering support inspire me daily.

To my powerhouse of a sister, Melanie J. Rego,
who founded ELEVATOR (elevatorinc.com), a "scrappy, bilingual public
relations agency," nearly 25 years ago in her Toronto apartment:
Your entrepreneurial vision and resilience are nothing short of extraordinary, Mel.

—Simon

"To lead and care for others, you must first care for yourself. *The Cognitive Behavioral Therapy Workbook for Leaders* is an effective resource for all leaders. In business, 'shit happens,' and many leaders are ill-equipped to deal with the challenges this puts on them, both personally and professionally. This book provides essential tools for all leaders to balance between a high-performance and high-care culture."

—**Calvin McDonald**, CEO of Lululemon Athletica Inc.

"*The Cognitive Behavioral Therapy Workbook for Leaders* is an essential resource for all leaders. It provides them with support for a range of issues (e.g., burnout, sleep, anxiety, anger, work-life balance, etc.) which are intrinsic problems which confront all leaders. The book fills a significant gap in the literature in addressing the personal care of our leaders in all walks of life. It is a must-buy for anybody in any kind of leadership role. Take the workout; you won't regret it!"

—**Cary Cooper, CBE, FAcSS**, professor of organizational psychology and health at ALLIANCE Manchester Business School, chair of the National Forum for Health and Wellbeing at Work, and coauthor of *Healthy High Performance*

"As leaders, the way we think shapes the way we lead. *The Cognitive Behavioral Therapy Workbook for Leaders* is a powerful, practical guide that helps you master your mindset, reframe challenges, and bring out the best in yourself and your team. If you're serious about growing as a leader, this book is a must-read."

—**Jairek Robbins**, performance coach and best-selling author

"This outstanding workbook offers solid psychological guidance for leaders in relation to their work and life. Throughout the workbook, the authors thoughtfully and purposefully weave theory, research, and practical guidelines. The reader is challenged to work at and use their thoughts, emotions, and behaviors as personal assets in their leadership roles. I recommend this workbook to leaders in sport organizations, business entities, health care, and educational systems."

—**Charles A. Maher, PsyD, CMPC, FAASP**, sport and performance psychologist for the Cleveland Guardians, professor emeritus of applied psychology at Rutgers University, and author of *Consulting in Sport Psychology*

"This workbook brings cognitive behavioral principles into the real world of leadership—skillfully going beyond mental health into issues of performance, stress resilience, and communication in the workplace. Rooted in classical cognitive behavioral therapy (CBT), it also reflects the spirit of newer developments—mindfulness, values, and emotional flexibility—but without straying from its strong, evidence-based foundation. A practical, science-informed guide for those who want to lead with psychological insight and behavioral skill. Highly recommended."

—**Steven C. Hayes, PhD**, Foundation Professor Emeritus of Psychology at the University of Nevada, Reno; and author of *A Liberated Mind*

"Leaders are more successful when they can effectively manage their own emotions and those of others, and this book is one of the best ways for leaders to learn how to do so. It draws on state-of-the-art techniques that have been rigorously evaluated. And, with many excellent case studies and exercises as well as lucid prose, the authors show how leaders can use these techniques to thrive."

—**Cary Cherniss, PhD**, emeritus professor of applied psychology at Rutgers University, and coauthor of *Optimal*

"Julian Barling and Simon Rego's *The Cognitive Behavioral Therapy Workbook for Leaders* is a concise, evidence-based guide that empowers leaders to manage stress, enhance decision-making, and foster resilience through CBT techniques. Its practical exercises are grounded in psychological rigor, offering actionable strategies for navigating leadership challenges. While very insightful, it also demands commitment to self-reflection. A must-read for leaders seeking mental clarity and emotional intelligence in high-pressure environments."

> —**Juggy Sihota**, senior vice president of TELUS Health

"The best leaders, first and foremost, are emotionally healthy humans. Healthy leaders foster more dynamic, thriving organizations. *The Cognitive Behavioral Therapy Workbook for Leaders* provides a comprehensive, evidence-based guide (utilizing CBT, dialectical behavior therapy [DBT], and acceptance and commitment therapy [ACT]) for those in charge to overcome mental health challenges and thrive in their leadership roles. An indispensable resource for leaders in every field."

> —**Matthew McKay, PhD,** coauthor of *Thoughts and Feelings* and *The Dialectical Behavior Therapy Skills Workbook*

"As a former student of Julian Barling, I always valued his incisive approach to leadership. This workbook profoundly applies that rigor to mental health, something that we need to pay more attention to in executive ranks. It's a vital guide for leaders navigating today's complex landscape, offering evidence-based tools to cultivate resilience and drive positive change."

> —**Steven Goldbach**, sustainability and infrastructure practice leader at Deloitte US

"The greatest leaders I've worked with that excel in high-pressure, high-impact roles relentlessly pursue the well-being *and* performance of their team (and themselves) to be able to sustain this achievement over the long haul. This book provides an excellent, evidence-based road map to accomplish this."

> —**Erica Wiebe, MBA**, Olympic Champion in freestyle wrestling, TEDx speaker, and manager of the Canadian Olympic Committee

"Barling and Rego combine their decades of expertise, beautifully synthesizing key principles of leadership with evidence-based mental health strategies. This practical and engaging workbook helps leaders prioritize their own mental health, and supplies them with easy-to-apply skills and strategies from CBT, DBT and ACT to effectively manage a range of challenging emotions and behaviors that impact both their work and personal lives. It's a must-read for current and future leaders!"

> —**Alec L. Miller, PsyD**, cofounder of Cognitive & Behavioral Consultants, LLP; and cofounder of the Access Psychology Foundation

Contents

Foreword   vii

Introduction   1

Chapter 1   Anger   11

Chapter 2   Anxiety   27

Chapter 3   Depression   43

Chapter 4   Burnout   61

Chapter 5   Romantic Relationships   77

Chapter 6   Sleep   95

Chapter 7   Substance Use   111

Chapter 8   Workaholism   129

Chapter 9   Work–Life Balance   145

Chapter 10   Moving Forward   159

Afterword   163

Acknowledgments   167

Resources   169

Endnotes   173

Foreword

The Cognitive Behavioral Therapy Workbook for Leaders is a practical guide that combines the science of leadership with the science of cognitive behavioral therapy (CBT). CBT was developed by my father, Aaron T. Beck, MD, over fifty years ago for the treatment of depression. Since that time, it has continually evolved and been adapted globally by clinicians and researchers. It has become the most widely studied and widely practiced psychotherapy in the world; thousands of research studies have established its efficacy for a wide range of mental health conditions and psychological issues.

The theory behind CBT is straightforward: It isn't situations that directly lead to a person's reactions. Rather, it is the meaning they put to situations, expressed in their thoughts (the words that go through their minds) that is more closely connected to how they feel emotionally and how they behave (and sometimes how their body responds). This theory doesn't just apply to people with a mental health diagnosis. It applies to everyone. Let me give you an example. You have just learned that one of your most trusted employees has gone to work for a competitor. If you think, "I can't believe they did this to me, after all I've done for them," you'll probably feel angry, and you might berate your staff for not predicting this outcome. If you think, "Oh, no, what if this turns out to be terrible for our business?" you'll probably feel anxious, and you might call an emergency meeting even though it's very late at night and could lead to panic among your employees. If you think, "We're definitely going to go out of business now," you might feel despondent and give up, instead of investigating ways to recover from this potentially major setback.

A key technique in CBT is learning to identify your thinking when you notice you are experiencing negative emotion, or you are acting in a way that is not useful. Another key technique is learning how to evaluate your thinking to see how accurate and helpful it is. If it is accurate, you need to do problem-solving. If it is not, you need to change your thinking.

Part of the evolution of CBT over time has been the inclusion of techniques from other evidence-based treatments. While this workbook teaches you to use a broad array of CBT techniques, it also includes techniques from dialectical behavior therapy (DBT) and from acceptance and commitment therapy (ACT)—for example, managing your feelings, using mindfulness to detach from unhelpful thinking, and engaging in valued actions. This combination of skills allows you to respond to your thinking so you can do better problem-solving, make better decisions, get a handle on your negative emotions, improve your relationships, and act in ways that are better for achieving your goals.

Leaders often believe they should be unshakable, immune to the struggles the rest of us face. But as research has shown time and time again, leadership brings its own set of challenges— stress, burnout, anger, anxiety, and even depression. Drawing on decades of clinical research, the authors have put together a guide that not only offers a better understanding of mental health but also provides tools to tackle those challenges. This book teaches that taking care of your mental health is not a sign of weakness; it is an essential strategy for better leadership. I've seen, both professionally and personally, how mastering these techniques can shift not just an individual's wellbeing but also the culture of an organization. When leaders embrace this approach, they create a work environment based on transparency, empathy, and proactive problem-solving. The impact can be profound: better decision-making, stronger communication, and a more resilient, engaged workforce.

I especially appreciate how the authors recognize the dual nature of leadership. It is a role with great responsibility, but it is also an opportunity for personal growth. Leaders who are willing to face their own vulnerabilities and reflect on their own development are more likely to inspire trust, empathy, and creativity in their teams. This workbook not only emphasizes the importance of self-awareness but also gives you the tools to develop the emotional and cognitive skills you need to thrive. By applying these practices to themselves, leaders invest in their own wellbeing, which ultimately benefits their teams and organizations. It's a win–win situation: a healthier leader equals a more dynamic, thriving organization. When you change the story you tell yourself, you change the world around you. This workbook embodies that wisdom, providing a clear road map for leaders to grow both professionally and personally.

As you work through this book, I encourage you to reflect on your own leadership journey. Think about the moments when adversity led to personal growth. Let these reflections inspire you to see mental health not as a destination but as an ongoing process—one that can enhance your leadership and your life. This book bridges the legacy of modern psychotherapy with the future of leadership, where self-awareness, resilience, and intentional action drive real change.

—Judith S. Beck, PhD
President, Beck Institute for Cognitive Behavior Therapy
Clinical professor of Psychology in Psychiatry, University of Pennsylvania

Introduction

Take nothing on its looks; take everything on evidence. There's no better rule.

—Charles Dickens, *Great Expectations*

Congratulations on choosing to read our book! It is clear that you are serious about being a wonderful leader and, at the same time, enhancing your wellbeing. Based on rigorous evidence that we will share, we believe that reading this book—and doing the exercises—will help you achieve these goals.

Becoming a leader often seems so enticing given the status, salary boost, and resources that you will receive. Yet holding an organizational leadership position is not for the faint of heart. As you well know, leadership comes with never-ending challenges that, if you're not careful, can negatively impact your mental health. Indeed, there are at least four factors that make leaders vulnerable to mental health problems.

The first is unrelated to your leadership position, but rather to the simple fact that you are *human*! Holding a leadership position does not make you immune to common mental health issues. The second is that other people hold high expectations of those in leadership positions, believing that they should be strong and able to weather whatever comes their way without wavering and without needing help. It's as if you are expected to be the sturdy lighthouse in a storm, even though we all know that even lighthouses need maintenance or they risk crumbling. Third, as a result, when leaders do experience mental health problems they may be stigmatized as weak and incompetent. Fourth, enacting quality leadership can be emotionally and cognitively taxing on leaders.

Recognizing these four factors lays the groundwork for understanding why leaders like you are just as predisposed to mental health challenges as anyone else in society. We start with a discussion of each of these factors. We then briefly review what we know about evidence-based psychotherapies and how they can be applied to the mental health challenges so many leaders face. In the chapters that follow, we identify the top nine mental health issues that can hurt your leadership, followed by specific, easy-to-use techniques to deal with each issue.

You may be asking yourself whether all this requires the help of a licensed professional, or whether you can develop useful skills just from reading our workbook. Fortunately, reliable studies have shown that *bibliotherapy*—the use of reading material and the exercises in a book such as this—can be as effective as working with a therapist for creating behavioral change,[1] may be more effective for people of working age,[2] and that gains made can last at least 6 months.[3]

Both of us have written other workbooks of this nature. Simon has written two extremely successful workbooks (*The 10-Step Depression Relief Workbook: A Cognitive Behavioral Therapy Approach* and *The CBT Workbook for Mental Health: Evidence-Based Exercises to Transform Negative Thoughts and Manage Your Well-Being*), which have since been translated into at least five other languages. In addition to working intensively with leaders for more than three decades and doing extensive research on leaders' mental health, Julian co-wrote *Positive Exam Results—Without Stress* more than 40 years ago![4]

Ready to get to it? Let's go!

Leadership and Mental Health

Let's look more closely at the four factors.

Factor #1: Leaders Are People Too

The prevalence rates for mental health disorders such as anxiety or depression tell us what we might expect for leaders. For instance, 20 percent of school principals experienced anxiety symptoms[5] and 11.5 percent of the general population experienced depression pre-COVID.[6] The situation becomes more dire when people experience two or more mental health disorders at the same time, which unfortunately occurs quite frequently; around half of people with anxiety also experience depression.

Factor #2: Others' Expectations of You as a Leader

Leaders also face challenges to their effectiveness that are unique to their organizational roles and responsibilities. Among those are perceptions and expectations that other people hold of leaders, which cause stigma toward leaders who deviate from these perceptions and expectations, and the paradox that doing whatever you can to be a wonderful leader is often very taxing and exerts its own emotional toll.

Most people have strong views on how ideal leaders should behave. These views develop well before they hold their first jobs or encounter their first organizational leaders. As Tiffany Keller showed in her research,[7] parents model behaviors to us early in our lives, and observing them shapes our beliefs about ideal leadership behaviors. Later on, teachers and celebrities also model leadership for us. By the time we are adults, we invariably have set ideas of how we expect ideal leaders to behave.

According to implicit leadership theories, people generally see leaders as sensitive, intelligent, dedicated, and dynamic,[8] all of which imply personal strength and wellbeing, and therefore people think leaders enjoy higher levels of wellbeing and lower levels of mental health problems, believing that people with mental health problems are less likely to be transformational leaders.[9] Leaders are assumed to have fewer mental health problems because of their greater access to job resources and job control.

Sadly, there is a real downside to these beliefs and expectations. Like all adults, leaders may inherit certain genetic vulnerabilities or may experience adverse child experiences that can predispose them to mental health challenges later in life. And when people's views of how their leaders *actually* behave deviates from their stereotypical views of how they *should* behave, the particular leader is likely to be judged negatively, even stigmatized, by those around them.

Factor #3: Stigma Against Leaders with Mental Health Issues

There's a concept called "leadership humble-bragging," by which we mean leaders who struggle with mental health challenges yet brag about them to others. One example is leaders who boast about just how little sleep they get,[10] despite the evidence that healthy sleep is essential for quality leadership (see chapter 6). Tom Ford, design director at Gucci, reportedly sleeps just 3 hours a night. He does not credit his success to talent, but to his energy. U.S. President Donald Trump not only once bragged about just sleeping for 3–4 hours per night, but also reportedly cannot believe how anyone who sleeps for 12 hours a night could be competitive. Former President Barack Obama also reportedly slept for just 6 hours each night. Other well-known leaders who are open about the fact that they sleep between 4 and 6 hours each night include Angela Merkel, Martha Stewart, Richard Branson, and Jeff Imalt. Articles in business journals such as "11 Successful People Who Get by on Hardly Any Sleep" don't help![11]

The implication is: I am an effective leader because I am impervious to mental health issues; if you are vulnerable and struggle, something must be wrong with *you* (you are weak or ineffective). And this is where stigma rears its ugly head.

Stigma is so pervasive and strong that even having easy access to mental health resources does not mean they will be used. A case in point would be Employee Assistance Programs (EAPs), which are usually open to everyone in an organization. Because of stigma, leaders are less likely to use EAPs or to seek any help from others. Even though those seeking this help are promised confidentiality, they may still fear the negative consequences of this information becoming known. It's easy to see that leaders probably have more to lose than employees if others learn of their difficulties and thus are more reluctant to use these services in the first place.[12] In addition, leaders who have risen from the ranks are often excluded from social interactions with their former peers, and fear of judgment from those former peers may make them more likely to hide their struggles instead of seeking their support.

All this has important consequences for leaders and their organizations. First, in a survey of just over a thousand global senior leaders during the pandemic, over half feared negative effects on their careers if others in the workplace learned of their mental health issues.[13] Second, when leaders withdraw from their followers, they feel lonely, while their followers question whether the leader can motivate them, help them be successful, make good decisions, and be effective. Third, humble-bragging does not work! Instead, it can lead to leaders being viewed as less competent and warm, and as a result less likely to receive help from coworkers when they need it most.[14]

Factor #4: The Double-Edged Sword of Being a Leader

We have long known that quality leadership is associated with employees' wellbeing.[15] But what about the effects on leaders' own wellbeing?

One large study in Germany investigated the effects of transformational leadership on leaders' own wellbeing.[16] Higher levels of transformational leadership were linked with higher levels of emotional exhaustion (the primary dimension of burnout; see chapter 4) two years later. Moreover, when leaders gained a lot of their self-esteem from their involvement in and attachment to the organization, the negative effects of enacting transformational leadership on emotional exhaustion were even higher.

Two studies from the United States found this happens[17] because transformational leadership is *emotionally taxing* on the leader, and that the effects were significantly higher when followers' competence was questionable—presumably because follower incompetence would deplete leaders' cognitive and emotional resources. A Chinese study found that being in charge of competent workers was satisfying for leaders, but psychological strain increased when leaders also had to meet the needs of others like their own leaders and peers.[18]

Finally, one of the major responsibilities of leadership is the need for business travel. While often viewed as a benefit of the position, the more people traveled for business, the more likely they were to suffer from anxiety, depression, difficulty sleeping, and excessive alcohol use.[19] Higher levels of business travel were associated with anxiety and depressive symptoms, and business travel over 21 nights in a month was likely to result in excessive alcohol use and difficulty sleeping. Business travel was also associated with higher body mass indices,[20] perhaps because of fewer opportunities for exercise and having to eat at restaurants and hotels.

Now that you're aware of the "big four" factors that leave leaders such as yourself vulnerable to mental health problems, ask yourself: do any (or all!) of these apply to you? If the answer is yes, the good news is that there are a number of practical tools derived from evidence-based psychological treatments that can address these mental health issues! But before we begin to help you to fill your toolbox, let's take a moment to "level-set" on what we know about these treatments and how they have the potential to help you.

Evidence-Based Psychological Treatments

We use the term *evidence-based* a lot in this book. Simply stated, it refers to treatments that have been proven to help by repeated high-quality research studies. In other words, there is plenty of evidence that the skills we describe work as intended, for what they are meant for, and that you can rely on them to work for you.

In the fast-paced and ever-evolving world of business, as a leader you need reliable data on your company's key performance indicators to drive organizational success. Whether analyzing market trends, team financial performance, or the efficacy of new strategies, data-driven decision-making can guide your way forward while minimizing risk. Wouldn't you want to use the same approach when it comes to addressing your mental health issues?

Fortunately, reliable data from rigorously performed research studies have determined the most effective psychological approaches for promoting mental health and wellbeing. While not everyone has the time or resources available to commit to seeing a psychologist, the good news is that these treatments can be delivered in other formats (such as workbooks like this one), which fit more easily into the typical lifestyle of leaders without sacrificing effectiveness—as long as you're committed to doing the work!

What Is the Evidence That Psychotherapy Works?

Many people still associate psychotherapy with Sigmund Freud and his writings in the late 19th and early 20th centuries. While Freud is widely considered the founder of psychotherapy, his method of *psychoanalysis* relied on what scientists call anecdotal evidence—personal stories or isolated examples—rather than the systematic collection of data as happens in most modern scientific research.

In the late 1990s, an emphasis on systematic scientific research to support decision-making in clinical, educational, medical, organizational, and policy contexts led to the development and use of evidence-based psychotherapies for the treatment of mental health conditions.[21] These methods have demonstrated *efficacy* (they produce the expected result under ideal circumstances) and *effectiveness* (they produce a beneficial result in real-world settings). Unlike traditional approaches, these newer interventions focus on the present, not the past. They are not rooted in conjecture, anecdotal evidence, or pseudo-science;[22] instead, they are supported by more than a half-century of empirical (that is, based on observations validated by repeated testing) evidence for a range of issues that people—including leaders—commonly face. As an added bonus, these newer treatments can not only alleviate symptoms and problems but increase quality of life, enjoyment, satisfaction, and wellbeing.

What makes these newer treatments even more valuable is that they are often as effective as taking medications for psychological issues in the short term and tend to remain effective long after treatment is completed. If people are already taking a medication for their mental health but still struggling, adding an evidence-based psychotherapy helps. By learning new techniques for coping, you not only can help yourself feel better today but will also be equipping yourself with skills that will help you cope better with tomorrow's problems—as long as you keep practicing!

Among the most rigorously researched and widely recognized evidence-based psychotherapies are cognitive behavioral therapy (CBT), dialectical behavior therapy (DBT), and acceptance and commitment therapy (ACT). All three are similar in that they focus on current thoughts, feelings, and behaviors; incorporate cognitive and behavioral techniques; and teach specific skills that promote healthier coping strategies to improve functioning and wellbeing. At the same time, these three evidence-based approaches differ in some core principles and components, focus, and strategies and techniques.

CBT was developed in the 1960s by psychiatrist Aaron T. Beck and is considered by many experts to be the gold standard of the psychotherapy field,[23] with more evidence for its effectiveness than any other psychological therapy.[24] CBT is structured and goal-oriented. It tends to focus on the present rather than delving into childhood events. CBT emphasizes the importance of the relationships between thoughts, feelings, and behaviors and offers practical skills to identify and challenge negative thought patterns, change unhelpful behavioral patterns, and better manage emotions. Because it offers practical, concrete strategies for addressing specific problems, CBT is particularly well-suited to the demands of leadership roles.

DBT was developed in the 1970s and 1980s by psychologist Marsha M. Linehan.[25] DBT helps people live in the moment, develop healthy ways to cope with stress, regulate their emotions, and improve relationships with others. DBT teaches mindfulness, emotion regulation, interpersonal effectiveness, and distress tolerance, enabling people to manage intense emotions while simultaneously working to change behaviors. Abundant evidence supports the effectiveness of DBT for individuals with a wide range of mental health issues.[26]

ACT was developed in the 1980s by psychologist Steven C. Hayes.[27] ACT helps people cultivate mindfulness, acceptance, cognitive "defusion" (that is, learning to detach and see thoughts as just thoughts, not facts), as well as commitment and other processes that increase psychological flexibility while promoting behavior changes consistent with personal values. Research consistently supports the effectiveness of ACT.[28]

CBT, DBT, and ACT are all effective and often produce comparable results.[29] Do certain elements from these approaches sound more appealing to you than others? The good news is that many of the "active ingredients"—the specific components and strategies—in these techniques work quite well on their own as well as when mixed and matched.

What's in It for You?

By embracing the notion that there are at least four big factors that can make you, as a leader, vulnerable to mental health problems, and then diligently working through the evidence-based techniques described in this workbook, you have the opportunity and ability to enhance your mental health—which in turn can assist you in becoming more like the leader you want to be! Whether it be anger, burnout, substance use, or another of the nine mental health issues discussed in this book, the strategies and skills derived from CBT, DBT, and ACT offer simple yet powerful strategies for overcoming them. Because we now know that leaders' mental health is important for effectiveness, this workbook can help you prioritize your own performance and mental health as you cultivate an empathetic and supportive culture where team members feel valued, understood, and empowered to thrive. And when that happens, other valued signs of leadership effectiveness, such as reduced absenteeism, increased productivity, and enhanced job satisfaction, will emerge.

Still not sold? On top of all this, CBT, DBT and ACT are cost-effective! Investing in evidence-based solutions for mental health issues isn't just the right thing to do, it's the smart thing to do. Addressing mental health concerns proactively is more cost-effective than dealing with the consequences of untreated conditions.[30] By allocating time and resources toward the evidence-based interventions in this workbook—which you can do wherever and whenever you choose—you will have at your fingertips all the tools you require to overcome and even avoid many of the barriers to good leadership.

How to Use This Book

The fact that you have reached the end of this section is great! It provides a high-level introduction to leaders' mental health and the evidence-based strategies you will find to help you deal with and overcome your own personal challenges.

You do not need to read every single chapter in this book to get the greatest benefit from it. Fortunately, we have never met any leaders who struggled with all nine mental health issues! Nor are the chapters presented in order of importance. So, feel free to bounce around the book, focus on those chapters of most interest to you, and come back to the book if another issue emerges down the road.

That said, while you do not have to read each chapter, there may be some benefit in doing so. Many of the same evidence-based techniques appear in different chapters. For instance, versions of cognitive restructuring exercises appear in every chapter, providing the opportunity to use the version that best suits your own challenges. To help you customize the concepts to fit your life, we've provided exercises and worksheets throughout that help you to identify and work with the issues most relevant to you.

If you wish to go beyond the material we provide, good for you! We've thought long and hard about the resources we include at the back of the book.

Moving Forward

Leaders are under enormous pressure! Not just to be contributing members of their families and societies but also to their organizations. Organizational leadership can be a joy with many rewards, but it also presents several barriers to mental health. You do not need to just sit back and accept these barriers. On the one hand, there are easily accessible interventions such as physical activity, contact with nature, and yoga that are not emotionally demanding and positively influence mental health.[31] On the other hand, as you will see throughout this workbook (remember, you can read the chapters in any order you want), you can learn and master techniques and strategies derived from evidence-based psychological treatments that will help you optimize your mental health and, in turn, maximize your effectiveness as a leader.

So, treat this workbook as your personal hardware store. Add the specific tools to your toolkit that you can use to maintain and enhance your mental health while you build a strong foundation for your leadership journey.

Good luck as you move toward being the leader you've always wanted to be!

—Julian and Simon

Chapter 1

Anger

Anybody can become angry—that is easy. But to be angry with the right person and to the right degree and at the right time and for the right purpose—and in the right way—that is not within everybody's power and is not easy.

—Aristotle

Possibly as a result of Freud's idea of *catharsis*—that venting intense emotion is beneficial—the role of anger in the workplace has long been controversial. After all, if Freud is correct about catharsis, surely having leaders venting their anger would be healthy for employees, teams, and leaders themselves? Sadly not!

As Aristotle reminds us, anger is extraordinarily complex. While often misunderstood as a purely negative emotion, anger can be adaptive when it motivates us to address injustices or protect ourselves from danger. (Think of the "fight" side of the "fight-or-flight" reaction that is built into your nervous system.) Problems only arise when anger is disproportionate to a given situation, persistent, or expressed in problematic or destructive ways. In these cases, anger can damage relationships, take a toll on medical and mental health, and lower overall quality of life.

Anger and Leadership

What about leaders' anger in the workplace? Not surprisingly, anger is the most studied of all the emotions in the leadership literature.[32] Some findings will seem obvious, while others may surprise you.

Schwartmüller and colleagues found that the more leaders expressed their anger by talking louder and quicker, showing angry facial expressions, openly stating they were angry, or swearing at, demeaning, or threatening employees, the angrier their employees became.[33] Angry employees were much more likely to reciprocate by making fun of or being rude to their leaders—hardly the behaviors that build leader effectiveness or a productive team environment.

Anger reduces leaders' effectiveness.[34] Essentially, employees spend time and emotional energy trying to make sense of their leaders' anger. The negative attributions employees make about angry leaders range from "they don't like me" to "they are racist/homophobic." While leaders might use anger to get their employees' attention or improve their performance, employees view anger as inappropriate, harmful, worthless, and an overreaction. They also view angry leaders as less competent, warm, or likable and may see them as lower in status and lacking self-control.

Would you be motivated to go above and beyond to make your organization thrive if you worked for a leader who was constantly angry? Probably not! In situations like this, people are more likely to seek revenge and retribution.[35]

Not every negative emotion has these effects; the quality of employees' relationships with their leaders was hurt when leaders displayed anger, but not when they displayed anxiety.[36]

REFLECTION EXERCISE 1.1
Your Experience of Anger at Work

How have you experienced a leader expressing anger toward *you* in the workplace? How did it affect your feelings toward that leader? Did it improve your overall performance or decrease it?

_____

_____

_____

_____

It's not just anger targeted directly at you that counts! Have you experienced a leader expressing anger toward a close colleague or peer in the workplace? How did it affect your feelings toward that leader? Did it improve your overall performance or decrease it?

_____

_____

_____

_____

How do *you* express your anger in the workplace? Does it affect your employees and their productivity? Does it improve your leadership quality or decrease it? How do you know?

_____

_____

_____

_____

_____

_____

The Nature and Amount of the Anger Makes a Difference

If anger is a natural human emotion that we are evolutionarily wired to experience, then it is not a feeling we can—or would want to—always avoid and eliminate. On the contrary, anger has been useful for our survival as a species for millennia and is still useful in certain situations today. It's the *nature* and *amount* of anger that makes a difference.

When anger is disproportionate to a given situation or becomes excessive or uncontrollable, it can quickly lead to problems in both your personal life and your leadership effectiveness. So, your task is to understand when and why you feel angry and then develop skills that will help you to manage it.

Anger is a complicated emotion, and leaders may express it differently depending on the situation. You may have heard the term "righteous anger"—or what we psychologists like to call "moral anger." In an experiment at a large Australian university, students read about a leader who was angry because an employee had exaggerated the benefits of an insurance policy either to increase his own sales (an integrity violation) or because of a lack of knowledge (a competence violation).[37] Anger because of an ethical violation increased perceptions of the leaders' effectiveness, while anger because of a competence violation decreased perceived leader effectiveness.

Why the difference? Reacting with anger to a lack of integrity not only signals to employees that such behavior is morally unacceptable, but it also increases the perception of the leader as effective. Reacting with anger to incompetence not only upsets employees, but it also causes them to perceive the leader as ineffective.

The *amount* of anger expressed by leaders is also important.[38] Low levels of anger and assertiveness can result in leaders being perceived as weak, while high levels can mean leaders are perceived as hostile and aggressive. Moderate levels of anger and assertiveness are often seen as appropriate.

CBT, DBT, and ACT for Anger

CBT, DBT, and ACT are highly effective approaches for managing anger. Each provides strategies and techniques to understand, challenge, and change anger-provoking thoughts, regulate your body's response to feeling angry, and decrease your anger-driven behaviors. To simplify things, we will use the CBT model for anger as our foundation.

The CBT Model of Anger

CBT is based on the premise that our thoughts, emotions, and behaviors are all interconnected. Anger typically is triggered by the interaction between an external event and our internal thought processes. These processes include our rules for living—beliefs about how people should or should not behave—which shape the way we interpret external events and drive our responses to perceived injustices or frustrations. In other words, to *feel* angry, we have to *believe* that someone has broken one of our rules for living. The amount of importance we place on the rule, the rigidity with which we hold it, and the perceived seriousness of the violation all influence the intensity of the anger, which can range from mild irritation or annoyance to full-on rage.

As is the case with all emotions, when we feel angry our bodies generate physiological sensations. For example, you may notice that your heart rate or breathing rate increases. Left unchecked, negative thoughts, emotions, and physiological sensations can then drive us to act in problematic ways, leading to further negative thoughts about the event (see Figure 1.1).

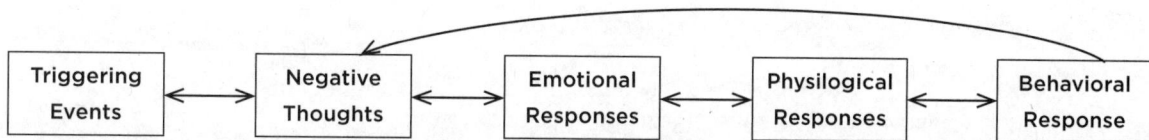

| Triggering Events | ⇄ | Negative Thoughts | ⇄ | Emotional Responses | ⇄ | Physilogical Responses | ⇄ | Behavioral Response |

Figure 1.1. CBT Model of Anger

CBT can help you to manage your anger in a number of ways, including becoming more aware of your triggers, learning how to identify and modify your negative (and often distorted) beliefs about the events that trigger and/or intensify anger, learning to better manage your emotional and physiological responses, and learning skills to replace anger-driven behaviors. In other words, if you can change the way you think about the triggering event and become better equipped to manage your emotional and physiological responses, you can develop more self-control and flexibility!

REFLECTION EXERCISE 1.2
Identifying Triggers

What triggering events—in the workplace or other areas of life—have you noticed tend to spark feelings of anger within you?

_____

_____

_____

_____

What are the typical thoughts you have when you are angry?

_____

_____

_____

_____

How and where do you experience anger in your body?

_____

_____

_____

_____

What do you typically do when you are angry?

_____

_____

_____

_____

The Key Components of CBT for Anger

CBT can be highly effective in managing anger,[39] using the following skills:

1. **Cognitive restructuring** helps you identify and challenge irrational or maladaptive thoughts that contribute to your anger. By replacing these thoughts with more rational and balanced ones, you can reduce the level of anger you feel when you think about the triggering event.

2. **Emotion regulation** (also a key component of DBT) helps you enhance your awareness of anger and the physiological response that goes with it, improving your ability to respond in healthier and more effective ways.

3. **Behavioral skills training** teaches you new ways of coping with anger-provoking situations, so that you will be able to adapt and respond appropriately when you feel angry.

Cognitive Restructuring

Cognitive restructuring is the cornerstone of CBT for anger management. Remember: it is not what other people do or do not do, but rather your thoughts about their actions that make you angry! Because you cannot control how everyone around you behaves, you are left with changing the way *you* think if you want to feel less angry.

Cognitive restructuring involves four steps. The first step is to learn to identify the situations and triggers that make you angry. Keeping a diary of anger episodes can help you to pinpoint these. You can practice doing this using the following worksheet.

REFLECTION EXERCISE 1.3
Diary of Anger Episodes

Use this diary to track anger episodes. Note the date, situation, trigger, thoughts, physical sensations, behaviors, and outcome of each episode. We provide an example entry.

Date	Situation	Trigger	Thoughts	Physical Sensations	Behaviors	Outcome
June 1	At work	Colleague ignored my input in a meeting	"She doesn't respect me." "She humiliated me."	Tense muscles, racing heart	Raised voice, left the room	Felt embarrassed, unresolved conflict

Once you have learned to identify your triggers, the next step is to identify any inaccurate and/or unhelpful thoughts. One quick and easy way to begin is to scrutinize your thoughts for any cognitive distortions that may be contributing to your feelings of anger. The following table gives examples of each, along with examples of how to correct your distorted thoughts.

Table 1.1 Common Cognitive Distortions and Their Corrections

Example Thought	Cognitive Distortion	Corrected Thought
"They always ignore me."	Overgeneralization	"They have responded in the past. Perhaps they are just busy and did not see my message."
"If I don't confront them aggressively, they'll walk all over me."	Catastrophizing	"I can address the issue calmly—I did so before with excellent results."
"They're such a jerk."	Labeling	"They might be having a bad day and didn't mean to be rude."
"I failed to keep my cool; I'm hopeless."	All-or-Nothing Thinking	"I lost my temper this time, but there are plenty of times when I've managed it well and I can use this as an opportunity to learn and improve."

After identifying inaccurate or unhelpful thoughts, the next step involves challenging these thoughts. Question the evidence for and against these thoughts, consider alternative explanations, and evaluate the usefulness of alternative perspectives versus your original beliefs.

For example, if you have the thought "they always ignore me," ask yourself the following questions:

- *Evidence:* What evidence do I have for (and against!) them always ignoring me?

- *Alternatives:* Could there be another reason they did not respond?

- *Usefulness:* Does thinking this way help me manage my anger?

The last step is to replace unhelpful thoughts with more balanced thoughts. This technique is also called *reframing*. It allows you to see the issue from another perspective. Instead of "they always ignore me!" a reframing thought could be "they might be busy," or "they might not have seen my message."

Using the triggers you identified above, do the following exercise to note the main unhelpful thought associated with each, challenge it, and then respond with a more balanced thought.

REFLECTION EXERCISE 1.4

Challenging Unhelpful Thoughts

Trigger	Unhelpful Thought	Technique Used to Challenge It	Practice Using the Technique	Balanced Thought
My colleague ignored me[40]	"He doesn't respect me."	Evidence for and against	Evidence for: He did not respond to my comment in the meeting. Evidence against: He usually responds to my comments. Plus he often asks my opinion in meetings and frequently selects me to take on important tasks.	"Maybe he was just preoccupied or didn't hear me. If he really didn't respect me, he would not turn to me so often."

Emotion Regulation

The second key ingredient in CBT (and DBT) for anger management is emotion regulation. Remember, feeling angry involves having both negative thoughts about the situation and a strong physiological response (the "fight" reaction). If you can learn to identify and manage your bodily reactions, you will feel more in control of your anger.

Here are four different emotion regulation skills you can practice. The key is to find an approach that resonates with you and that is easy to practice on a daily basis!

Mindfulness involves focusing your attention on the present moment and observing without judgment. Becoming more aware of your thoughts, feelings, and bodily sensations allows you to create a little space or distance between a feeling and your response, which can lead to more proactive behaviors. In other words, mindfulness provides you with an opportunity to recognize when you are starting to feel angry earlier, and then either take steps to prevent the anger from escalating or choose a more constructive response to it. Many people find it easiest to start with mindful breathing. However, there are an endless number of ways to practice mindfulness and countless excellent resources out there to help you. One good place to start might be with Jon Kabat-Zinn's classic book listed in the resources section at the end of the book. Because of mindfulness's robust utility and benefits, we revisit it in many of the chapters that follow.

Progressive muscle relaxation involves sequentially tensing and then relaxing different muscle groups in your body. Most people start with their head and neck and work down, but you can start with toes/feet if you prefer. Tense and hold each muscle group for a few seconds before releasing. Doing so helps make you aware of what it feels like to be tense, as well as what it feels like to manually reduce the physical tension in your muscles. Then when starting to feel angry you can focus on relaxing muscles that are tense, which can reduce the intensity of your anger and help balance your thoughts. Again, there are many different ways to practice progressive muscle relaxation and dozens of excellent resources for learning it.

Deep breathing helps activate your body's relaxation response, toning down the part of your nervous system that fires the fight-or-flight response and reducing the intensity of bodily sensations, which in turn reduces feelings of anger and helps rebalance thoughts. One well-known, simple technique is diaphragmatic breathing. To do this, practice taking deep "belly" breaths, inhaling through your nose for a count of four, holding for a count of four, and exhaling through your mouth for a count of four. Repeat this process several times and observe how you feel. Ideally, practice it when you are not angry so you can really feel how it helps you relax. Then you'll be more confident in your ability to use it when you start to feel angry.

Time-out involves disrupting feelings of anger by temporarily escaping from the triggering event. Stepping away from the situation, engaging in a calming activity, and then returning when you feel more in control can provide you with some time to allow your emotions to diminish, which should help you approach the situation more rationally.

To maximize effectiveness, these techniques can and should be combined with the cognitive restructuring techniques we covered in the previous section, as well as with the behavioral skills training techniques described below.

REFLECTION EXERCISE 1.5
Plan for Managing Angry Feelings

List the different ways you aim to address feelings of anger next time they arise. For example, "I will step away from the situation and engage in deep breathing. If I still feel dysregulated, I will..."

_____

_____

_____

_____

_____

_____

_____

Behavioral Skills Training

We all have different strengths and weaknesses. Through no fault of our own, we also sometimes lack certain skills that others have been gifted with. (Think of math, singing, athletics, and so forth.) The same is true for anger management! Some people need to learn new behavioral skills to manage their anger more effectively and constructively. Two of the most common behavioral approaches are assertiveness training and problem-solving.

Assertiveness training teaches you to express your needs and feelings openly and respectfully, without resorting to verbal or physical aggression. This is an especially important lesson if you struggle with assertiveness. Table 1.2 shows how to tell when you are being appropriately assertive.

Table 1.2 **Contrasting Assertiveness, Aggression, and Passivity**

Aspect	Passive	Aggressive	Appropriately Assertive
Communication Style	Quiet, hesitant, avoidant	Loud, harsh, disrespectful	Calm, clear, respectful
Goal	To avoid conflict or discomfort	To dominate or intimidate	To express needs and opinions
Impact on Relationships	Leads to misunderstandings and unmet needs	Damages relationships, creates fear and resentment	Improves understanding and respect
Example Statement	"It's okay, my opinion doesn't really matter."	"You never listen to me, and it's demeaning and infuriating!"	"I feel upset when my input is ignored."
Emotional Impact	Leads to feelings of resentment and helplessness	Increases stress and guilt	Promotes self-respect and reduces stress
Behavioral Outcome	Avoidance and internalizing anger	Conflict escalation and hostility	Constructive problem-solving
Self-Perception	Low self-esteem and lack of control over situations	Regretful or justified by anger	Confident and in control

Problem-solving teaches you how to approach issues with a calm, rational mind. The following exercise takes you through the steps of problem-solving.

REFLECTION EXERCISE 1.6
Problem-Solving Steps

1. Define the Problem You Experience

Example: *I feel angry when my ideas are ignored in meetings.*

_____

_____

_____

2.   Brainstorm Solutions

Example: *Discuss the issue directly with my team member.*

Example: *Write down my ideas and send them via email.*

_____

_____

_____

3.   Evaluate the Pros and Cons of Each Solution

Example: *Discussing directly clarifies misunderstandings but can be uncomfortable.*

Example: *Emailing ideas ensures they are received but lacks immediate feedback.*

_____

_____

_____

4.   Choose the Best (or Easiest) Solution

Example: *Discuss the issue directly with my team member.*

_____

_____

_____

5.   Implement the Solution

Example: *Plan to talk to my team member after the next meeting.*

_____

_____

_____

6. Review the Outcome

Example: *My team member listened to me and agreed to ask for my ideas at the next meeting. I was nervous but I felt better after we talked.*

• *Case Example: Applying CBT for Anger Management*

Jon is a 35-year-old man with chronic anger issues. After being passed over several times, Jon has recently been promoted to a junior leadership position in his organization. He often finds himself getting angry at work, especially when he feels excluded and disrespected by team members and peers. This has started to interfere with his ability to lead his team.

Jon began keeping an anger diary to track his anger episodes so that he could identify and understand the triggers, thoughts, and behaviors associated with his anger.

Using cognitive restructuring, Jon identified a recurring thought: "When my team members don't listen to me, I feel really disrespected." He was concerned that this would hurt team effectiveness. Jon challenged this thought by exploring alternative explanations and the evidence for and against his belief. With practice, over time, Jon began to adopt more balanced thoughts, such as "Maybe they are busy or distracted," "Their behavior is not necessarily about me," and "Perhaps I should check in with them and ask how they are doing."

Jon taught himself simple mindfulness techniques from a reputable site on the internet and began to incorporate a 5-minute mindfulness practice into his daily routine. He learned to observe his emotions without immediately reacting to them, giving him more time and control in choosing how he wanted to respond. Jon also decided to learn some relaxation techniques on his own, so he downloaded a recording of deep breathing instructions, which he practiced daily and then started to use when he felt his anger rising.

Jon focused on improving his assertiveness and problem-solving skills. He learned to express his feelings calmly and constructively, using "I" statements instead of accusatory language. For example, instead of saying, "You never listen to me," he practiced saying, "I feel frustrated when my ideas are not acknowledged during our meetings."

Over several months, Jon felt a significant reduction in his anger episodes. He felt more in control of his emotions and noticed improvements in his relationships with his team members, and his team members responded with improved communication and engagement.

Conclusion

Anger management is not just about eliminating or suppressing anger, but rather about understanding and expressing it constructively. If you find yourself experiencing excessive anger or have difficulty controlling it, you can transform your anger from something destructive into a catalyst for positive change using the tools and strategies that we have just described. Through cognitive restructuring, emotion regulation, and behavioral skills training, you can become a more effective (and respected) leader!

Chapter 2

Anxiety

No amount of anxiety makes any difference to anything that is going to happen.

—Alan Watts

Being a leader involves high stakes, immense responsibilities, and constant scrutiny. Each of these factors can generate anxiety; together they can form a "Bermuda Triangle," catching you in a swirl of anxiety that can impact your effectiveness. To combat this, you need to understand what anxiety is, where it often shows up, and what you can do to manage it.

Although it may not feel like it, anxiety can be an extremely helpful emotion—under the right circumstances! In our early history as a species, anxiety's primary function was to keep us safe from dangers in our environment (like saber-toothed tigers hanging around outside the cave). The problem is that while our society has evolved a great deal since then, our brains have not. Anxiety still has one main task: to protect us from threats.

And that is a problem, because the emotional center of our brain does not differentiate between physical threats like someone attacking us and social threats, such as being judged negatively by others. Nor does it consider whether these threats are real or imagined, or whether they are present right now or may (or may not!) happen in the future. Once you *perceive* something as threatening, your brain triggers your nervous system to activate its "fight-or-flight" mode. Your body experiences a cascade of physiological changes that are meant to prepare you to immediately defend yourself (fight) or get out of harm's way (flight). While this "alarm reaction" is helpful if you're about to be mugged, it's not so helpful when you're reacting to something that may or may not be true in the moment, or about something that may or may not happen in the future. Even worse, this "alarm reaction" is known to randomly misfire for no good reason from time to time. Every year up to 11 percent of people in the United States experience a panic attack, and an estimated 28 percent of the population will experience at least one in their lifetime.[41]

While a number of different factors can account for why you might be *predisposed* to feel anxious (such as genetics, early life stressors, childhood trauma, or medical conditions), for many reasons this predisposition may lie dormant and unnoticed until *precipitated* (triggered) by a key, often stressful workplace event, such as a new boss or downsizing. Note: even *positive* events such as a long-sought-after promotion can cause anxiety!

Once activated, anxiety may take any number of forms. For many leaders, it may take the form of decision-making anxiety, such as worrying about making the wrong choices, uncertainty about potential changes at work, high standards (your own or others'), or a lack of confidence in your own leadership performance. Once present, anxiety can be triggered in any number of ways and is often perpetuated by your thoughts and actions.

REFLECTION EXERCISE 2.1
Understanding Your Anxiety

Use this opportunity to identify the factors that influence your anxiety.

Predisposing Factors

Do you have any family history of anxiety? Do you have any personality traits that might make you vulnerable to anxiety? Think about any challenging early life experiences that might contribute to your anxiety.

_____

_____

_____

_____

Precipitating Factors

Think about any recent changes (negative or positive) in your life that may have triggered the onset of your anxiety. When did your anxiety start? When did it become a problem in your life?

_____

_____

_____

_____

Forms

Which form(s) of anxiety fit you?

_____

_____

_____

_____

Triggers

Under what circumstances do you currently experience anxiety? When you are at home? At work? When alone? When having a meeting with your team members? Your boss? Being tired? Stressed? Hungry?

_____

_____

_____

_____

Perpetuating Factors

What might be keeping your anxiety going? What do you tend to do when you are anxious? What do you tend to think? Are these things actually helpful, or could they be reinforcing or maintaining your anxiety in the long term?

_____

_____

_____

_____

Anxiety and Leadership

A study of nearly nine thousand teachers across the United States (teachers are leaders too!) elicited that 1 in 5 had an anxiety disorder.[42] Teachers with an anxiety disorder were much less satisfied with their jobs, experienced less control at work, took almost twice as many sick days per month, and were more likely to quit the organization within a year. They were also 50 percent more stressed and had a lower quality of life than those who did not have an anxiety disorder.

As you probably know for yourself, anxiety can be depleting, sapping you of the emotional energy and concentration you need for quality leadership. It's like a slow leak in your car's gas tank; you may not realize just how much it drains you until you have nothing left to run on. One consequence of this is that anxiety is avoidance;[43] the more leaders reported feeling anxious, the less their subordinates viewed them as active and engaged leaders.[44]

It makes sense that anxiety could cast a shadow on being a good and especially a transforma- tive leader, as being an ethical, inspirational, and relational leader takes considerable energy. It is not surprising that according to another large study in the United States, leaders' anxiety was indeed associated with significantly lower levels of transformational leadership.[45]

When you feel really anxious, you probably have less energy and patience for dealing with challenging team members or spearheading a difficult project or new initiative. Small provoca- tions are often enough to make you overreact to what might otherwise have been easily ignorable issues. This does not make you a bad person; it just confirms that you are human. Mary Mawritz and colleagues were among the first to document that anxiety was positively associated with behaviors such as ridiculing team members or telling them they are stupid.[46] The same pattern of findings were seen among both American and Chinese leaders.[47] Leaders do not just snap at random employees when they are anxious; they are far more likely to do so with poorly perform- ing employees, which might cause those employees to perform even worse.

People who feel anxious often notice that their heart starts to pound or their pulse seems to race. Terry Szuplat, a member of President Obama's speechwriting team, provided excellent advice for people about to give a presentation that might be useful if you are feeling anxious before heading off, for example, to a meeting with a difficult employee or a budget meeting with a demanding director.[48] Szuplat recommends that when practicing the presentation, do jumping jacks first. This can help you become accustomed to the bodily sensations associated with anxiety so you can learn to tolerate it. In CBT, we call this type of exercise "interoceptive" exposure. Why does this work? By simulating the physical symptoms of anxiety through jumping jacks, you can learn to "decatastrophize" those sensations as nothing more than background noise—they are no longer distracting.

Szuplat's advice also reminds us of the importance of practice. If you are actively involved in any sports, you will know the incredible benefits of practice before a big event or competition. Practicing for a high-stakes meeting is just like rehearsing for a big game. You wouldn't compete without training, so why take on tough employees, customers, or bosses without preparation?

CBT, DBT, and ACT for Anxiety

What else can you do to help combat anxiety and restore some of the physical and mental energy that it drains? CBT, along with DBT and ACT, offers many useful tools for this. Cognitive restructuring, exposure, mindfulness (also in DBT and ACT) and relaxation, and behavioral activation offer practical strategies to help leaders cope with their anxiety, ensuring they can lead with greater confidence and clarity.

Cognitive Restructuring

If you read chapter 1, you know that cognitive restructuring involves recognizing and then altering inaccurate and/or unhelpful thinking patterns. Common cognitive distortions that leaders with anxiety may experience include catastrophizing, dichotomous (black-and-white or "either/or") thinking, and overgeneralization. By catching these and other distortions, and then learning to reevaluate and restructure your thoughts, you can develop a more rational and balanced perspective, which should in turn decrease your anxiety. You may want to take a look at Exercise 4.1 in chapter 4 for a list of common cognitive distortions and how to reframe them.

Exposure

Exposure means facing situations that you know provoke your anxiety and that you have deliberately been avoiding. Common anxiety-provoking situations for leaders include public speaking, difficult conversations, making high-stakes decisions, and networking. The key here is to begin to face your fears gradually and systematically. Gradually means that you ease in, one step at a time, starting with less potent fears. Systematically means that you continue to make efforts to confront rather than avoid these situations, with the goal to keep moving up your hierarchy of feared situations until you are able to tackle the ones you fear most.

The first step is to develop a log of your anxiety triggers. Take a moment to think about your current anxiety triggers and rate them from 0 (none) to 10 (max). Then arrange them from the least to most anxiety-provoking.

REFLECTION EXERCISE 2.2
Your Anxiety Exposure Hierarchy

List the situations you tend to avoid, with a rating from 0 (none) to 10 (high) of how anxious they make you.

Situation	Anxiety Level (0–10)

Engaging in gradual and systematic exposure to the situations on your list not only helps to reduce avoidance (a key perpetuator of anxiety) but also creates new opportunities for learning and building resilience—all of which increase your confidence and lessen your anxiety associated with these situations. Table 2.1 provides examples of exposure exercises.

Table 2.1 **Examples of Gradual and Systematic Exposure Exercises for Leaders**

Public Speaking	Start by speaking in smaller, supportive settings like team meetings before moving on to larger audiences.
Difficult Conversations	Role-play with a trusted colleague or coach before actually engaging with the difficult person(s).
Decision-making	Start by making smaller, less risky decisions independently. Gradually work up to higher-stakes choices.
Networking	Begin by attending informal gatherings with peers and then progressively engage in larger, more formal networking events.

Mindfulness and Relaxation

Mindfulness involves focusing your attention nonjudgmentally on what is happening in the present. Relaxation involves engaging in body-focused exercises to decrease stress and tension. These are often paired; for instance, you can use mindfulness to disengage from anxiety-provoking thoughts while using relaxation exercises to promote a sense of calm.

One of the biggest myths about mindfulness and relaxation is that you need to devote hours a day to them to see a benefit. Nothing could be further from the truth! The impact of both can be felt with just a few minutes of daily practice. Like any new skill, however, the key to success is persistent practice. Think you are too busy? Table 2.2 offers some examples of mindfulness and relaxation techniques that you can easily fit into your day.

Table 2.2 Examples of Helpful Mindfulness and Relaxation Techniques

"Micro" Mindfulness (2–5 minutes)	Between meetings, focus on your breathing. As you inhale and exhale, notice and let go of any thoughts that enter your mind and just return to your breathing.
Body Scan at Your Desk (3–10 minutes)	Sit comfortably and mentally scan your body from head to toe. Notice any areas of tension and consciously relax them.
Diaphragmatic Breathing (1–3 minutes)	Inhale slowly through your nose for 4 counts, inflating your belly. Hold for 4 counts. Exhale slowly out of your mouth for 4 counts, deflating your belly. Hold for 4 counts. Repeat for 1–3 minutes.
Mindful Walk (10 minutes)	During a break, go for a brief walk and focus your attention outward—the sensation of your feet on the ground, the sights and sounds and smells in the environment around you.
Intentional Transitions (1–2 minutes)	At the end of a workday, spend 1–2 minutes sitting quietly and reflecting nonjudgmentally on the day. Use this as a buffer to transition from work to your personal life.
Grounding Exercises (30 seconds) This quick way to ground yourself during moments of high stress is borrowed from DBT.	Practice the 5-4-3-2-1 technique: Name 5 things you see, 4 things you feel, 3 things you hear, 2 things you smell, and 1 thing you taste.
Cognitive Defusion (1–2 minutes) This technique for changing your relationship with your thoughts is borrowed from ACT.	Instead of just thinking a thought (for example, "I must be perfect"), try instead to think, "I'm noticing that I'm having the thought" (in this case, "I'm noticing that I'm having the thought that I must be perfect"). This reduces the thought's power.

We suggest you keep a log of your mindfulness and relaxation practice sessions. A sample log is provided in Table 2.3. Rank your anxiety levels before and after each session. Note successes and challenges in the reflection column.

Table 2.3 Log of Mindfulness and Relaxation Practice

Date	Time	Exercise Practiced	Time Spent (min.)	Anxiety Before (0–10)	Anxiety After (0–10)	Reflection

You can also try using one of the many mindfulness apps for guided mini-meditations. If you don't know where to start, MIND (mindapps.org) offers an interactive database that can help you find mental health apps that meet your unique preferences and needs.

Behavioral Activation

Behavioral activation involves increasing your engagement in activities that bring a sense of pleasure or enjoyment while doing them, and a sense of mastery or accomplishment afterward—even if anxiety makes it challenging to do them. Anxiety often leads to avoidance, which, as you are already aware, only reinforces negative emotions and perpetuates withdrawal. Behavioral activation can help to break this cycle by having you reconnect with activities that align with your values, which in turn can increase feelings of meaningfulness, self-efficacy, and confidence—and thus decrease feelings of anxiety. See Table 2.4 below for some examples.

As with mindfulness and relaxation exercises, the goal is to find opportunities during your busy day and week for some of these activities. Although it may seem counterintuitive to plan these sorts of activities when you are already so busy, incorporating small, manageable activities into your routine can create a positive feedback loop that helps to improve your mood and reduce your anxiety. In turn, learning to successfully manage your anxiety will make you feel more confident and be more effective as a leader, which will make you want to keep doing these activities!

Table 2.4 **Behavioral Activation Examples**

Activity	Specific Examples
Short-Term Wins	Schedule a 10-minute task that feels manageable, like reviewing one portion of a report. Completing it can build a sense of mastery and momentum.
Wellness Breaks	Plan a daily 15-minute walk outdoors. Bonus: Pair with mindfulness to maximize its impact.
Reconnecting with Past Hobbies	Dedicate 30 minutes a week to a hobby you once enjoyed but have stopped doing because you are "too busy," such as playing an instrument, gardening, or reading.
Team Member Reinforcement and Engagement	Set aside time each week to informally connect with team members. For example, catch someone doing something well and compliment them, or celebrate a small win together.
Exercise	Dedicate 30 minutes 3–4 times a week to some form of exercise.

Take a moment to write down your own list of possible activities.

Bonus: Values Clarification and Committed Action

Values clarification and committed action are considered essential components of ACT. They also align seamlessly with the behavioral activation principles of CBT. For you as a leader, identifying your core values—such as integrity, collaboration, or innovation—can provide a compass for decision-making and a sense of purpose and direction, even in the face of anxiety. These values can then serve as a foundation for committed action, in which you deliberately choose to take steps aligned with what truly matters to you rather than being driven by your anxiety. For example, if you value collaboration, you might prioritize open communication with your team even when feeling anxious or vulnerable.

When integrated with behavioral activation, values clarification and committed action can help ensure that the activities you choose are not only mood-enhancing but also personally meaningful, reducing anxiety and enhancing leadership effectiveness.

What matters most to you? If you're unsure, the following values clarification exercise can help you identify and connect with your values—that is, the things that are truly meaningful to you. This exercise can also help you to distinguish between socially imposed expectations and personally significant principles. Clarifying your values can then serve as a road map for *committed action*, which involves translating your values into concrete, achievable steps. Doing so can enhance your ability to persist in meaningful behaviors despite obstacles that may appear along the way, fostering behavioral change despite discomfort.

REFLECTION EXERCISE 2.3
Values Clarification

Step 1: Sit in a quiet space and reflect on moments of pride or fulfillment in your leadership role and in your life.

_____

_____

_____

Step 2: Identify any recurring values (for example, "collaboration" or "integrity" or "family") in these moments of pride or fulfillment.

_____

_____

_____

Step 3: Create goals that better align your daily actions at work and/or at home with these values.

_____

_____

_____

Step 4: Practice committed action by identifying and taking concrete steps toward your goal despite discomfort.

_____

_____

_____

Step 5: Return to this reflection exercise and note how it went, how it felt, and what you learned.

_____

_____

_____

• *Case Example: Applying CBT for Anxiety Management*

Shireen is a 35-year-old director in a rapidly expanding commercial architectural company. Shireen had been experiencing anxiety over decision-making and interpersonal interactions for the past 6 months. The anxiety affected her sleep, personal relationships, and overall wellbeing.

Shireen's first step was to monitor her thoughts. Working with her executive coach, she identified two cognitive distortions (catastrophizing and overgeneralization) present in her most anxious moments. For example, Shireen often thought, "If I don't get this just right, everything will fall apart" and "I can't handle challenges! I am always going to fail at everything."

Once Shireen learned to identify her cognitive distortions, she practiced replacing them with more balanced thoughts like an engineer would with a weak bridge, exchanging weaker beams for stronger beams that could withstand the pressures of leadership. For example, she practiced thinking, "I can handle challenges as they come; one mistake won't ruin everything."

Shireen started approaching the triggers for her anxiety head-on, rather than avoiding them. She created a list of all her current triggers, rated them from 1 to 10, and arranged them from least to most anxiety-provoking. She then began to face them gradually and systematically, starting with the least anxiety-provoking. Shireen gradually built up her confidence to approach the ones at the top. Interestingly, she learned that as she engaged in exposure, her ratings began to decrease for all the items on her hierarchy, even the ones she had not yet faced!

Shireen also created a new routine to fit mindfulness and relaxation into her busy life. She started the day with either a 5-minute body scan or mindful breathing exercise, took a 10-minute break at midday to do either a mindful walk or relax between meetings, and began doing an evening wind-down routine where she would use either progressive muscle relaxation or breathing exercises to decompress. As a bonus, Shireen also practiced taking a 5-minute pause to reflect on her values before making any major decisions and applied mindful listening techniques during social interactions at work to reduce social anxiety and enhance interpersonal connections.

In addition, Shireen began to monitor her daily activities, which gave her a better idea of where her time was going and, more importantly, where she might fit in activities that weren't work-related. Next, she created a list of activities that she predicted would give her a sense of pleasure or mastery. She then looked for openings in her schedule where she could incorporate activities from the list. She realized that she could get off the subway or bus one stop early and walk the remaining way to work, doing the same on her trip home. She also began to listen to podcasts on the trip home, rather than answering emails.

Finally, Shireen spent time identifying her core values, which included collaboration and employee wellbeing at work and health and family outside work. She began to be more deliberate about aligning her actions with these values, such as by fostering a supportive work environment and encouraging creativity among her team members, as well as increasing exercise and reaching out more to family.

Over time, Shireen felt significantly less anxious. She also became more flexible in her thinking, made better decisions, and led her team with greater confidence and clarity.

Conclusion

Anxiety does not define you or your ability as a leader, but how you respond to anxiety certainly can. Remember, the goal is not to eliminate anxiety. Instead, the tools in this chapter can help you lead with even greater clarity and confidence, despite what your anxiety might be doing. By recognizing your thought patterns and challenging unhelpful beliefs, as well as clarifying your values and then committing to behaviors that are aligned with them, anxiety can become a catalyst for transformational leadership and help you model psychological flexibility and vulnerability for your team.

Chapter 3

Depression

I have sometimes had a feeling of being pursued by a "black dog"—it was a feature of my youth. I did not like standing near the edge of a platform when an express train was passing through.

—Winston Churchill

In a fascinating but controversial book entitled *A First-Rate Madness*, psychiatrist and researcher Nassir Ghaemi offers a counterintuitive perspective on the possible effects of depression on leadership behaviors.[49] Contrary to what most might expect, Ghaemi not only suggests that experiencing a depressive disorder could improve leadership quality, but that depression may be a *necessary precondition* for good leadership.

First, Ghaemi suggests that depression is associated with higher levels of realism. However, he then complicates the matter by suggesting that only certain levels of depression result in greater realism, while too little or too much depression could lead to distorted or illusionary thinking. He backs up this idea by referring to Churchill's long-standing battles with depression. He hypothesizes that Churchill could be so successful as a leader in World War II and understand that Hitler was never going to compromise because *his* depression enabled him to see the threat posed by Hitler in a realistic manner. (He argues that Neville Chamberlain failed to appreciate Hitler's intentions precisely because Chamberlain was mentally healthy.)

The second reason Ghaemi offers is that depression causes people to be empathic, and empathic leaders draw on their prior experiences of depression to enhance their leadership. He refers to the many great military heroes and political leaders who suffered major depressive episodes at various points in their life, including U.S. General Sherman, President Lincoln, Mahatma Gandhi, and Martin Luther King Jr.

Oprah Winfrey, American talk show host, television producer, actress, author, and media proprietor, who twice taught the sought-after course *The Dynamics of Leadership* to MBA students at Northwestern University and has often been ranked as the most influential woman in the world, has also been open about her own struggles with depression.

These hypotheses rely on what we might regard as post hoc or backward thinking. In other words, we can only offer these hypotheses *after* the event. The best way to gather evidence would be to track leaders with depressive disorders and see if their leadership changed for the better or worse. Second, and equally important, cherry-picking (also known as the logical fallacy of incomplete evidence) by telling inspiring stories about the difficult lives that only some wonderful leaders have had, while ignoring great leaders who suffered no depression or leaders whose depression may have overwhelmed their leadership, provides a flimsy basis for evidence.

Despite these concerns, empathy is good for leadership, and for both relational and task-oriented leadership.[50] So, what is the evidence about the effects of depression on leadership behaviors?

Depression and Leadership

As we were writing this book, we could only locate one pertinent research project. Alyson Byrne and colleagues focused on the effects of depressive symptoms (rather than clinical diagnoses of depression) on three different forms of leadership in American leader–follower dyads.[51] A feature of this study is that because people rarely have a single mental health disorder, but usually have at least two—a phenomenon known as *comorbidity*—they also investigated what happens if depressive symptoms co-occur with symptoms of anxiety, as well as with alcohol consumption at work.* This is important, as approximately 85 percent of people who experience depression also experience anxiety.[52] People with major depressive disorders also have a 40 percent lifetime probability of having an alcohol use disorder.[53]

As expected, people who reported feeling depressed, even if they had not been diagnosed as having depression, were less likely to demonstrate transformational leadership and were more likely to be abusive to those under them. These problems were worse in those who drank more at work and in those who had higher levels of anxiety.

Putting this all together, the question of the effects of depression on leadership requires a more nuanced answer. While Byrne and colleagues found there is an indeed an effect on some leadership behaviors when depression occurs together with anxiety or alcohol use, their research was based on leaders who self-report depressive symptoms. People whose symptoms would warrant a diagnosis of major depression may have even more trouble at work.

This conclusion needs to be tempered by an understanding of the prevalence of depression symptoms. The *Household Pulse Survey* put out by the Centers for Disease Control states that one out of every three American adults has symptoms of depression or anxiety in a given week.[54] Given the number of people—presumably leaders as well—who experience depressive symptoms, the link with poorer leadership should be of concern to us.

CBT, DBT, and ACT for Depression

The greatest glory in living lies not in never falling, but in rising every time we fall.

—Oliver Goldsmith

We know that leaders are human just like everyone else, which means they are no more immune to depression than anyone else in society (see the introduction). Fortunately, CBT, DBT, and

---

* Intriguingly, as we will see in chapter 7, alcohol researcher Michael Frone (2013) counsels that we focus on alcohol consumption *at work*, as it has stronger effects on workplace behaviors than general alcohol consumption.

ACT offer practical tools that can mitigate the symptoms of depression and have the potential to increase transformational leadership, decrease abusive supervision, and improve decision-making and creativity. If you've been struggling with depression, let's explore how these techniques can help you—as a person and as a leader.

Cognitive Restructuring

As with anger and anxiety, cognitive restructuring can help you identify and challenge negative or unhelpful thoughts and beliefs and then replace them with more balanced and realistic ones, which leads not only to improved mood but also increased resilience and improved coping skills.

Recognize your automatic negative thoughts

Depression often is associated with the presence of "automatic" negative thoughts, which can pass through your mind without you even noticing, but nevertheless skew your perception of your leadership, your work, your team, and your future. As a result, the first key task in cognitive restructuring involves increasing your awareness of your thoughts and deciding whether they are helpful or not.

Scrutinize and challenge problematic or unhelpful thoughts

Once you have identified an unhelpful thought, the goal of cognitive restructuring is to find ways to alter it and make it more realistic. By practicing this skill regularly, over time you can develop the habit of reframing unhelpful thoughts as they arise, which should help reduce the negative thinking patterns that are often associated with depression.

But how do you challenge your thoughts? We describe several of the more common techniques throughout the chapters in this book. The most important thing to remember is that it all starts with your willingness to consider that how you're seeing or thinking about things may not be entirely accurate (and certainly not helpful).

One common cognitive restructuring technique involves putting an unhelpful thought "on trial."

REFLECTION EXERCISE 3.1
Putting Your Thoughts on Trial (Challenging and Changing Depressive Thoughts)

Step 1: Write down the depressive thought.

_____

_____

_____

_____

Step 2: Record the _evidence_ that both supports and disputes the depressive thought. And remember: Just as would be the case in an actual legal trial, evidence will only be accepted into the deliberations if it is verifiable. No opinions, guesses, or hearsay allowed!

_____

_____

_____

_____

_____

_____

Step 3: Become the "judge" and come to a fair verdict regarding your thought. Is it accurate? Objective? Are there alternative thoughts that could more accurately and reasonably explain the situation? If so, write them down.

_____

_____

_____

_____

Given that continual practice is essential if cognitive restructuring is to help change your dysfunctional thought patterns, take this opportunity to practice identifying any depressive thoughts you have as a leader, putting the thoughts on trial by providing evidence that supports or refutes them, and then coming to a fair verdict (generating a more balanced alternative). Table 3.1 provides an example.

Table 3.1 **Example of How to Challenge and Change Depressive Thoughts**

Depressive Thought	Supporting Evidence	Disputing Evidence	Balanced Thoughts
"I'm a failure as a leader."	*I made a poor decision that cost my team a big opportunity.* *I received negative feedback on a recent project.* *My team is struggling, and I feel responsible.*	*I have led projects successfully before.* *I have lots of positive feedback from colleagues, supervisors, and direct reports.* *One setback is not enough to define me as a complete failure.*	*"I have made mistakes as a leader, but many great leaders face setbacks and grow from them."* *"I have a track record of past successes. I can learn from this experience and improve."*

Behavioral Activation

People experiencing depression frequently feel a decrease in motivation and energy, which in turn often leads to decreases in activity (and vice versa!). From a leadership perspective, this means potentially engaging less with employees, peers, and supervisors, which collectively results in laissez-faire or passive leadership. The list of negative outcomes associated with passive leadership is long (and positive outcomes perhaps nonexistent).[55] Fortunately, behavioral activation can help you restore your leadership style by breaking the cycle of avoidance and withdrawal that perpetuates depressive symptoms. In essence, behavioral activation involves slowly and deliberately planning activities back into your life that you predict could bring you a sense of pleasure and joy and/or accomplishment and mastery—even when you do not feel like doing anything and your mind is telling you that nothing will help. Before making any changes, however, a good first step is to monitor your current level of activity.

Activity Monitoring

Activity monitoring will help you become aware of how you are currently spending your time each day, and the impact (or lack thereof) of these activities on your mood and leadership. By tracking daily activities and rating your associated pleasure and mastery, you can identify patterns of withdrawal or inactivity and begin to see opportunities for re-engagement. For example, you might discover that your workdays are filled with activities associated with low pleasure and mastery, like hiding in your office and just keeping up with routine tasks such as emails. Similarly, you might discover that your evenings and weekends are filled with activities associated with low pleasure and mastery, such as excessive television viewing or isolating yourself from friends and family. In contrast, tasks like connecting with team members, engaging in creative brainstorming, or spending time with family and friends often yield much higher ratings of pleasure and accomplishment than people with depression predict when their mood is low. Thus, activity monitoring lays the foundation for making targeted changes in your behavioral patterns.

The following table provides an example of how you can monitor your daily activities. Write down at least three activities per day and be sure to rate each of them on the following two dimensions: Pleasure (0–10) and Mastery (0–10). An example is provided.

Table 3.2 **Activity Monitoring**

Sunday	Monday	Tuesday	Wednesday	Thursday	Friday	Saturday
Brunch with family *(P 10, M 1)*	*Practiced mindfulness before starting the day* *(P 4, M 8)*	*Led team meeting* *(P 5, M 8)*	*Listened to podcast on way to work* *(P 7, M 8)*	*Spent a few moments in reflective prayer* *(P 7, M 8)*		*Ski trip* *(P 8, M 6)*
Watched football game *(P 8, M 2)*	*Delegated agenda items to team* *(P 10l, M 8)*	*Completed client report* *(P 5, M 10)*			*Completed quarterly report* *(P 7, M 9)*	*Apres-ski in lodge* *(P 10, M 2)*
Went for a walk *(P 5, M 8)*	*Left work early to have dinner with family* *(P 9, M 2)*	*Pickleball* *(P 8, M 7)*	*Date night* *(P 6, M 2)*	*Watched a ball game* *(P 8, M 0)*	*Went out for social hour with colleagues* *(P 8, M 3)*	*Played board game with family* *(P 7, M 2)*

Sunday	Monday	Tuesday	Wednesday	Thursday	Friday	Saturday

Activity Scheduling

Once you have monitored your activities for a week or two, you will have enough data to begin activity scheduling. The goal here is to deliberately increase your engagement in activities that give you a sense of pleasure and/or mastery but you don't seem to do very often anymore. Because your motivation will likely be low at the start, the task is to plan and commit to activities that you used to do (or have never done) that you predict will give you a sense of pleasure or mastery. Ideally, these activities will also be value-based (see the "Values-Based Activities" section later in this chapter, and the core values clarification exercise in chapter 4). Doing this will help you reduce time spent on activities that offer little or no pleasure.

REFLECTION EXERCISE 3.2
Brainstorming Ideas for Activities That Can Enhance Your Mood

Step 1: Identify activities from your activity monitoring that provide a sense of pleasure and mastery and also align with your core leadership values.

Step 2: Take a moment to brainstorm any additional activities that in the past have given you a sense of pleasure and/or mastery, as well as any activities that you have never done but that you predict could give you a sense of pleasure and/or mastery. You might call this your behavioral activation bucket list. Remember to consider all of your five senses when brainstorming; think of things you like to look at, listen to, smell, taste, and touch. Answering these questions for yourself will help get you started:

What are you currently doing that you could do even more of during the week?

_____

_____

_____

What have you stopped doing that you would like to pick up again?

_____

_____

_____

What are some things you've never done but always wanted to?

_____

_____

_____

Step 3: Use this information to start scheduling some of these activities into your week. Add them in small, manageable steps to ensure you do not feel overwhelmed; you are more likely to persist if you give yourself a chance to experience small, successive wins. For example, if the idea of hosting a full team meeting is daunting, start by scheduling brief, one-on-one check-ins with employees. If you used to love jogging during lunchtime, start by scheduling a walk outside every other day for half an hour.

Step 4: After completing each activity, rate your sense of pleasure and mastery from 0 to 10. What did you learn?

Step 5: Gradually increase the frequency and complexity of these activities as your confidence and mood improve.

Bonus: Reenergize and Reconnect with the 10:5 Rule

Organizational psychologist Ryan Fehr offers some practical advice he calls the 10:5 Rule that fits nicely with behavioral activation. His advice could be especially beneficial if you have been feeling sad and lonely yet have withdrawn and are spending more time alone in your office or even avoiding people when you walk around.[56]

What is the 10:5 rule? If you pass by anyone in the organization and they are within 10 feet, acknowledge them by making eye contact, with a smile or a hand gesture. If you walk within 5 feet of someone, say something as simple as "hi" and make eye contact. You will likely be amazed at how you reconnect with them, and they with you!

Problem-Solving

Depression often causes leaders to feel overwhelmed and stuck when tackling complex issues. As mentioned in chapter 1, problem-solving helps leaders break down challenging tasks into manageable steps, fostering an increased sense of work-related confidence, self-efficacy, and accomplishment.

Step 1: Define the problem. Break the issue into clear, specific, sequential, and actionable components. For example, instead of thinking "the team is never productive," you might realize that "team meetings usually lack clear objectives."

Step 2: Brainstorm potential solutions. Be creative and avoid self-criticism during this step. Generate a list of as many possible actions as you can, without initially judging their feasibility. For example, you might come up with "establish a meeting agenda," "delegate leadership for components of the meeting," or "emphasize the meeting goals."

Step 3: Weigh the pros and cons of each potential solution. Consider resources and time available and alignment with your values as a leader. For instance, delegating leadership might empower the team but also might require initial training.

Step 4: Choose the solution you think would be the easiest or most viable option and create a step-by-step plan to execute it. This might include providing necessary training, assigning tasks, setting deadlines, and scheduling check-ins to monitor progress.

Step 5: Evaluate the outcome. Reflect on whether the solution effectively addressed the problem. If not, return to step 2 and revisit the brainstorming phase to explore alternative approaches. Continuous evaluation fosters adaptability and growth.

Do not try to do this in your head! Taking the time to write out these steps makes the tasks much more powerful, effective, and doable.

Table 3.3 Applying Problem-Solving Skills

Define the Problem	Potential Solution	Weigh the Pros & Cons	Chosen Solution	Evaluate the Outcome
I have lost contact with my team.	*The 10:5 Rule.*	*Pro: Simple to do; forces me out of my office.* *Con: Awkward at first.*	*The 10:5 Rule.*	*Reconnecting with team members; feel less alone; team climate improving.*

Define the Problem	Potential Solution	Weigh the Pros & Cons	Chosen Solution	Evaluate the Outcome

By systematically approaching, rather than avoiding, complex challenges and breaking them down into manageable steps, you can regain confidence in your decision-making abilities, enabling a sense of self-efficacy and accomplishment. This will help reduce the feelings of help-lessness and hopelessness and low self-efficacy that are often associated with depression. Issues often become more challenging over time. Gaining these problem-solving skills and having confidence in how to use them can enable you to intervene early, before a problem becomes more complex. Problem-solving is not only a skill for more easily addressing the complex issues in your life but also fosters resilience by cultivating a proactive mindset.

Integrating ACT into the CBT Approach

When feeling depressed, it can be difficult to see your thoughts as distorted, which makes challenging them seem inauthentic. Fortunately, ACT offers many helpful techniques designed to increase your psychological flexibility in the face of emotional challenges like depression. Two key *acceptance* processes from ACT are mindfulness and defusion. As we note in other chapters, mindfulness encourages you to stop avoiding, fighting, or suppressing your thoughts and instead simply acknowledge and observe them without judging them. Defusion encourages you to mentally step back and distance yourself from your unhelpful thoughts by considering them to be just words or mental events rather than absolute truths. Both processes aim to reduce the influence your thoughts may be having on your actions, which allows you to engage in meaningful actions rather than getting stuck in rumination and avoidance.

In addition, ACT proposes that values guide meaningful actions in our lives, even or especially during challenging times; activities that are values-driven help provide direction and motivation, while also counteracting avoidance and increasing behavioral activation by encouraging small achievable actions. All these techniques can reduce feelings of aimlessness and break through the inertia that is a feature of depression.

Here are some exercises to build your skills in each of these processes. (Note: There is also a values clarification exercise in chapter 4 you may want to look at.)

REFLECTION EXERCISE 3.3
Becoming Mindful of Your Emotions

Step 1: Sit in a quiet space, if possible, with your eyes closed.

Step 2: Notice any emotions you are feeling and describe how they feel. For example: "I feel sad. It's like a heaviness in my body and a sense that I am about to cry." Do not judge them or try to change them.

Step 3: Observe your emotions as their intensity changes over time.

Step 4: Use a metaphor to help you detach. You might visualize your emotions as a cloud in the sky or a leaf floating by on a stream.

REFLECTION EXERCISE 3.4
Defusion: Labeling Thoughts

Step 1: Notice and acknowledge an unhelpful thought. Become aware of the thought as it pops into your mind without immediately reacting to it. Instead, simply observe that it is there without getting caught up in its content or emotional weight. Don't try to change it.

Step 2: Label it as a thought. For example, if the thought, "I'm a bad leader" arises, you would label it as a thought thusly: "I'm having the thought that I'm a bad leader" or "My mind is telling me that I'm a bad leader." This creates a little mental distance between yourself and the content of the thought. Can you see the difference?

Step 3: Let it be. Allow the thought to "do what it wants to do" without holding onto it, trying to challenge or change it, or trying to push it away. Just observe it, as you would the cars of a passenger train going by or objects moving on a conveyor belt.

Values-Based Activities

People experiencing depression frequently withdraw from activities they once found enjoyable or that gave them a sense of accomplishment. Fortunately, behavioral activation helps improve mood not only by increasing activities of pleasure and mastery but by offering leaders the opportunity to reconnect with their professional and personal values and reintegrate meaningful activities that align with their values back into their lives.

Values-based activities can include:

- Develop healthier patterns of eating, exercise, and sleep

- Reach out to employees, one by one, and offer to mentor them

- Reach out to friends or spend more time with family

- Volunteer for a cause

- Participate in a professional development workshop or conference

Capturing these in a simple chart like the one below can help you learn about patterns and see progress as it occurs. Use the blank chart on the following page to start your own plan.

Table 3.4 Values-Based Activities

Activity	Core Value	Planned Day/Time	Reflection
Team brainstorming	Fostering innovation	Wednesday 2 pm	Felt productive
Lunch with a mentor	Professional growth	Friday 12 pm	Inspired and connected
Volunteering event	Community engagement	Saturday 10 am	Felt a sense of purpose
The 10:5 Rule	Respecting others	Monday 10–11 am	It felt good; I felt less alone

Activity	Core Value	Planned Day/Time	Reflection

• *Case Example: Amanda's Leadership Journey*

Amanda, the 42-year-old CEO of a mid-sized health insurance company, began experiencing depressive symptoms after an important initiative she had led failed. She doubted her abilities, avoided key meetings, and started to disconnect from her team. Amanda's executive coach introduced techniques derived from CBT, DBT, and ACT to address these challenges.

Encouraged by her coach, Amanda began by identifying unhelpful negative automatic thoughts like "I'm incompetent" and practiced cognitive restructuring by generating more realistic and balanced alternative thoughts she could use to replace them. She also learned how to "put her thoughts on trial" by documenting evidence of her past successes to counterbalance her negative self-perception.

Amanda also practiced mindfulness by visualizing her self-doubting thoughts as passing clouds and defusion by labeling her thoughts as such ("There goes my mind again, telling me I'm incompetent") in order to create distance between herself and the content of her thoughts, especially when she was struggling with challenging her thoughts.

Amanda then engaged in activity monitoring for a week, which revealed that she had been withdrawing from opportunities to collaborate with her top management team and professional networking events—activities that she had previously found fulfilling and meaningful. With guidance from her executive coach, Amanda began activity scheduling, starting with small steps like using the 10:5 Rule and reaching out to a trusted colleague for a casual conversation.

After beginning with small, value-driven steps, Amanda again took on larger projects, like leading a new product development initiative, which reconnected her with her leadership mission.

Finally, Amanda used problem-solving techniques to address specific issues about her leadership that she learned from her failure. For instance, when her top management team was disengaged, she defined the problem, brainstormed solutions, and implemented the chosen strategies. Over time, the team's engagement improved, reinforcing her confidence.

After six months, Amanda's mood improved, and she reported feeling more connected to her team and confident in her leadership. She credited the combination of CBT's structured techniques and ACT's values-based approach for helping her recapture who she wanted to be as a leader.

Conclusion

Depression among people in leadership roles poses unique challenges, but by using tools derived from CBT, DBT, and ACT, leaders can maintain their effectiveness. Psychological flexibility results from identifying negative thought patterns and then either challenging them or distancing from them, increasing commitment and engagement in value-based actions that enhance a sense of pleasure and mastery, and learning to problem-solve issues as they are detected and before they become complex. Leaders can learn how to approach their depressive symptoms rather than escape from them or avoid them, reinvigorate their wellbeing, and enhance their leadership as well as the prospects for organizational success!

Chapter 4

Burnout

Great leadership involves creating an environment where people can do their best work sustainably. Recognizing and addressing [your own] burnout is part of that equation.

—Satya Nadella, CEO of Microsoft

Some people question whether burnout is real. The answer is yes! While not listed as a mental disorder by the American Psychiatric Association, burnout is viewed as an "occupational phenomenon" by the World Health Organization (WHO).[57] WHO now recognizes three different dimensions of burnout:

- Emotional exhaustion—feeling emotionally drained, depleted, and exhausted, which can result in insufficient energy to face work, and even a sense of dread about work.

- Depersonalization (or cynicism)—a negative and cynical attitude toward those you care for and diminished empathy and engagement, as a result of which you devalue and depersonalize clients or colleagues.

- Reduced professional efficacy—feelings of a lack of self-confidence and competence (lowered self-efficacy) about your work, which leaves you doubting whether you make a difference in your job.

WHO's definitions are consistent with Maslach and Jackson's Maslach Burnout Inventory (MBI).[58] Examples from the MBI convey the flavor of these three dimensions: "I feel used up at the end of the workday" (emotional exhaustion), "I've become more callous toward people since I took the job" (depersonalization), and "I deal very effectively with the problems of my recipients" (reduced professional efficacy: items on this dimension are reverse-scored). All convey the experience or feeling of burnout.

WHO and the MBI view burnout as a process. Emotional exhaustion develops first; if this is not taken care of, feelings of depersonalization and cynicism toward those for whom you are responsible can develop. Detaching from employees or treating them impersonally can then lead to reduced professional efficacy. The prevalence of emotional exhaustion is invariably higher than depersonalization and reduced efficacy,[59] which means that early interventions focused on emotional exhaustion could well prevent depersonalization or reduced professional accomplishments in the first place.

Emotional exhaustion among inexperienced leaders is more malleable than that among experienced leaders.[60] Interventions targeted at reducing emotional exhaustion may be even more useful in this group. Similarly, offering leadership training and development before leaders assume their first significant leadership position may be most useful for preventing burnout in the first place.[61]

Most research has focused either on emotional exhaustion or burnout as a whole. There is also much speculation that levels of burnout have risen after, and because of, the COVID-19 pandemic.[62] Burnout has been a major part of almost every discussion about work since the dark early days of COVID-19.

In one study, 20 percent of school principals have experienced emotional exhaustion.[63] Other estimates suggest that the rate of burnout is more than 50 percent among practicing physicians[64] and public health professionals.[65] The prevalence of burnout is greater than other mental health problems such as anxiety or depression (see chapters 2 and 3).

Burnout and Leadership

A large study of mid-level managers and employees at a Fortune 500 company has demonstrated the link between developmental challenges and emotional exhaustion.[66] The extent to which leaders faced developmental challenges (for example, job transitions, creating change, dealing with difficult employees) was associated with higher levels of emotional exhaustion, measured with the MBI.

Higher levels of emotional exhaustion often predicted whether leaders became passive or laissez-faire leaders. As mentioned in the previous chapter on depression, laissez-faire leadership is associated with a long list of negative effects, including poorer employee attitudes (hence, lower satisfaction and loyalty), motivation, performance, and wellbeing, as well as heightened employee ambiguity, uncertainty, and deviant behaviors such as employees calling in sick when they are not sick, and more workplace bullying and safety incidents.[67]

However, emotional exhaustion by itself does not necessarily result in laissez-faire leadership. This finding highlighted the critical role of belief in self-efficacy. People who believe they have efficacy are more likely to initiate action when appropriate and then persist at the task for longer.[68] Organizational challenges are unlikely to result in emotional exhaustion when leaders have confidence that they can meet tasks such as communicating with and motivating their employees and building team spirit. When leaders lacked belief in their own efficacy, organizational challenges were far more likely to result in emotional exhaustion.

While our initial goal should always be to build workplace environments that prevent leaders from feeling emotionally exhausted in the first place, effective interventions for improving one's own sense of self-efficacy can be useful.[69] We'll talk about such methods in the next section.

CBT, DBT, and ACT for Burnout

Almost everything will work again if you unplug it for a few minutes, including you.

—Anne Lamott, American novelist

As noted, burnout starts with emotional exhaustion—the feeling of being utterly drained by your responsibilities. Left unaddressed, this state can result in you seeing those people for whom you are responsible as "units" or "things" (depersonalization), which can then hurt your leadership effectiveness and result in a diminished sense of accomplishment. CBT, DBT, and ACT offer practical tools to help you lead with your values, become more mindful, regulate your emotions, and restructure your unhelpful thoughts. In doing so, you can avoid becoming enmeshed in activities that are disconnected from your values and lead to emotional exhaustion. Leading with your values may even help you prevent the burnout cycle from starting in the first place.

Figure 4.1 graphically presents the burnout process and the roles that values clarification, mindfulness, emotion regulation, and cognitive restructuring can play in disrupting it. The burnout process itself is presented in bolded boxes. As you can see, values clarification could help you reduce your feelings of emotional exhaustion. If you are already emotionally exhausted, cognitive restructuring, emotion regulation, and mindfulness exercises can help intervene and prevent emotional exhaustion from leading to depersonalization, and later on to diminished leadership quality. Let's delve into how you can achieve this.

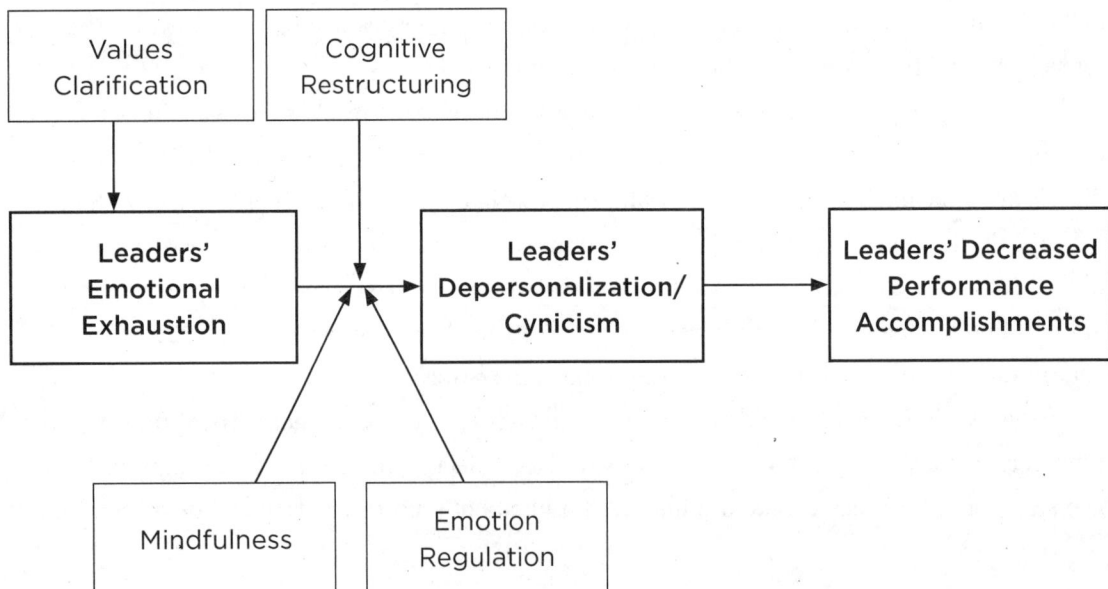

Figure 4.1. **Intervening in the Burnout Process**

Key Components for Burnout

CBT focuses on identifying and challenging negative thoughts and changing maladaptive behavioral patterns in order to achieve emotional relief and enhanced wellbeing. DBT combines CBT with mindfulness and emotion regulation skills to manage intense emotions. And ACT focuses on accepting difficult thoughts and emotions while committing to value-based actions. We will use one key component from each approach to illustrate how you can disrupt the burnout process: cognitive restructuring, emotion regulation, and mindfulness.

Cognitive Restructuring

A dysfunctional thought record (DTR) is a common tool used in CBT to help identify and challenge unhelpful thoughts and feelings about a situation. Learning to develop and use DTRs can help you recognize when your thoughts are unhelpful, so that you can challenge and reframe them in different ways to reduce the likelihood of emotional exhaustion.

Here are the five steps involved in creating a burnout-based DTR:

Step 1: Write down the situations linked to feelings of emotional exhaustion.

Step 2: Note the main thought in your head (such as "I have been avoiding the petty interpersonal conflicts in my team, and I could lose my job") connected to your feelings of emotional exhaustion.

Step 3: Search for cognitive distortions (like catastrophizing or all-or-nothing thinking) in the thought.

Step 4: Develop more balanced thoughts, such as "Ignoring inconsequential interactions doesn't define who I am as a leader; it may even make me a better leader."

Step 5: Reflect on emotional and behavioral changes.

Table 4.1 **Example DTR**

Situation	Automatic Thought	Cognitive Distortions	Balanced Thought	How I Feel Now and What I Will Do
Missed deadline	*"I'll be fired"*	*Catastrophizing*	*"One deadline doesn't define me"*	*Feel less anxious. Will notify the team and prioritize getting the task done. Will work on improving my organizational skills.*
Negative feedback	*"I'm a terrible leader"*	*Overgeneralization*	*"Feedback helps me improve"*	*Feel less depressed and hopeless. Will thank the team member for providing feedback, look at it as an opportunity to grow, and implement changes based on it.*

One of the most common cognitive distortions is *catastrophizing*—assuming the worst-case scenario. This is common in leaders experiencing burnout. Familiarize yourself with the cognitive distortions listed in the following exercise and use it to develop balanced thoughts.

REFLECTION EXERCISE 4.1
Counteracting Your Cognitive Distortions

Cognitive Distortion	Description of Cognitive Distortion	Examples of Cognitive Distortion	Possible Balanced Thoughts
Catastrophizing	Assuming the worst-case scenario	*I missed an important deadline; I will never be forgiven*	

Cognitive Distortion	Description of Cognitive Distortion	Examples of Cognitive Distortion	Possible Balanced Thoughts
Overgeneralization	Drawing broad conclusions based on a single negative event	*I made a mistake on this project; I'll never succeed as a leader*	
All-or-Nothing Thinking	Viewing situations in black-and-white terms, without recognizing the nuance or spectrum between extremes	*If I don't succeed perfectly in this role/assignment, I'm a failure*	
Mental Filtering	Focusing exclusively on the negative aspects of a situation while ignoring the positives	*My entire presentation was terrible because I stumbled over one answer*	
Disqualifying the Positive	Rejecting positive experiences or feedback as unimportant or invalid	*The team's praise doesn't count; they're just being polite*	
Mind Reading	Assuming you know what others are thinking, with a negative bias	*My team thinks I'm incompetent because I couldn't answer that question immediately*	

Cognitive Distortion	Description of Cognitive Distortion	Examples of Cognitive Distortion	Possible Balanced Thoughts
Fortune Telling	Predicting the future negatively without evidence	*If I take a vacation, everything will fall apart*	
Personalization	Taking responsibility for factors beyond your control	*The team's low performance is entirely my fault*	
"Should" Statements	Rigidly adhering to self-imposed rules or expectations that may not be realistic	*I should always be available to solve problems immediately*	
Magnification or Minimization	Exaggerating negatives while downplaying positives	*The one criticism from my boss really means I'm failing, even though the rest of my review was good*	
Emotional Reasoning	Believing that feelings reflect reality	*I feel overwhelmed, so I must be incapable of handling this role*	

Identifying and addressing cognitive distortions can help correct negative thought patterns, which can in turn reduce emotional exhaustion and hopefully stop the burnout process.

Over time, exercises like generating a personal DTR can also help you to automatically take a more helpful perspective. Remember, the more you practice this, the better you will get at it.

Cognitive restructuring and challenging negative beliefs are not the only tools at your disposal. If you're having trouble with challenging and reframing your thoughts, an equally powerful option is to practice emotion regulation.

Emotion Regulation: STOP!

The **STOP** skill (**S**top, **T**ake a step back, **O**bserve, **P**roceed mindfully) is an emotion regulation tool taught in DBT. It can be useful for leaders experiencing emotional exhaustion, as it helps them pause and create space before reacting impulsively. With time and practice, this skill allows leaders to regain control over their emotions and make more thoughtful decisions.

Stop. When you're feeling emotionally exhausted or your emotions seem to be out of control, the first step is to pause. Don't react. Pausing for a moment helps prevent you from being driven by your emotions and acting without thinking. Instead, take a moment to ground yourself, which will give you time to reflect rather than react. Stay in control. Remember, you are the boss of your emotions!

Take a Step Back. When you are feeling emotionally exhausted and are facing a difficult situation, it may be difficult to think about how to deal with it in the moment. Mentally or physically distance yourself from the situation to gain perspective. Move to a quiet space and take a few slow, deep breaths to help center yourself and give yourself some time to calm down and think. Rarely do we need to make split-second decisions about anything, so remind yourself that it is okay to take your time to decide how you want to respond.

Observe. Observe what is happening in the moment within you—your thoughts, feelings, and physical sensations—without judgment. Notice the thoughts, feelings, and sensations but don't allow yourself to jump to conclusions or get swept up in them. Instead, gather the relevant facts so you can understand what is going on and decide what options are available to you.

Proceed Mindfully. Stay calm and in control and choose a response that aligns with your values and long-term goals, rather than reacting impulsively or out of frustration.

Ask yourself what you want from the situation or what you could do to make this situation better. Remind yourself that it's okay to take some time to think things through.

Thought Watching

If you are new to mindfulness, an excellent exercise to start with would be "thought watching," which has you focus solely on observing your thoughts without attempting to reframe or change them in any way. Thought watching teaches you to detach from negative thoughts and observe them as transient events, reducing their emotional grip on you. This can lead to more productive behaviors and help prevent or reduce emotional exhaustion.

Step 1: Find a quiet moment. Sit comfortably. If possible, close your eyes. Take a few deep breaths to center yourself.

Step 2: If a negative thought arises, simply acknowledge it without judgment. Remember the earlier exercise on noticing your thoughts and say to yourself, "Here's a thought about how I am failing as a leader," or "There's a thought about the project being completed on time."

Step 3: Visualize the thought as a metaphor. For example, imagine placing the thought on a leaf floating down a stream, or as a cloud drifting across the sky, or a balloon rising into the air. Watch it move away at its own pace without trying to deliberately push it along, just like you would a leaf on a stream, a cloud in the sky, or a balloon in the air.

Step 4: Bring your focus of attention back to the present and your breathing. If (when!) the thought returns, simply repeat the process. If you notice feelings of frustration, it likely means you are trying to push the thought away or trying to prevent it from returning. Remember, your task is to simply notice it without judgment and then return to the present and your breathing.

The more you practice the mindfulness skill of thought watching, the easier it becomes and the more you will benefit from it.

Values Clarification

Emotional exhaustion and burnout can stem from being disconnected from your personal and leadership values. Most of us find ourselves being absorbed at different times in activities at work that just create no value; sadly, leaders are no exception. Whether it is an interpersonal conflict that is really quite inconsequential or human resource issues that other specialists could deal with more competently, these activities can drain us, and in doing so can start the burnout process. ACT emphasizes psychological flexibility in leadership—accepting difficult emotions while committing to meaningful actions aligned with your core values.

Reconnecting with What Matters

The following values clarification exercise is a straightforward yet powerful tool to help you to identify your core values, assess how well your behavior as a leader aligns with those values, and create meaningful steps to close any gaps between the two. Values clarification helps foster a sense of purpose and direction and allows you to (re)connect with what truly matters to you—which in turn can help to reduce, even prevent, feelings of emotional exhaustion and burnout.

Without a clear sense of values, leadership can feel like being lost in a dark dense forest, not knowing where to turn; clarifying your values can help light the way forward. It is all too easy to lose ourselves at work, becoming focused only on what seem like immediate crises and external pressures, resulting in feeling lost, overwhelmed, and emotionally exhausted. Knowing your values and letting them guide your behavior can help you prevent emotional exhaustion from occurring in the first instance, or at the very least reduce the severity of its impact on you and stop it from turning into depersonalization.

REFLECTION EXERCISE 4.2
Identify Your Core Values

Step 1: Start by reflecting on *areas of life* that matter most to you. Here are a few examples of categories to consider (and there are many online resources that can help as well).

- *Leadership*: What kind of leader do I want to be?

- *Relationships:* How do I want to show up for others?

- *Personal Growth:* What traits or skills do I need to develop?

- *Health and Wellbeing:* How do I want to care for myself?

- *Legacy and Contribution:* What impact do I want to leave when I am no longer with this team or organization?

Step 2: Write down 3–5 values for each area of life that matter most to you. For example:

- *Leadership: Transparency, fairness, inspiration*

- *Relationships: Supportiveness, empathy, honesty*

- *Personal Growth: Curiosity, resilience, self-awareness*

Area 1 (specify)

_____

_____

_____

_____

Area 2 (specify)

_____

_____

_____

_____

Area 3 (specify)

_____

_____

_____

_____

Step 3: Define what your values look like in action. First, list a value from step 2 above. Next, for each value, describe the specific behaviors or actions that would unambiguously reflect the value. You might make a grid like this:

Value	Behavior or Actions	Alignment Rating (1–10)
Fairness	*Treat all employees based on their performance*	

Step 4: Assess the alignment of your values and behaviors. Rate on a scale of 1–10 how well your current actions align with each value. As an example, if fairness is the value, rate "How often do I ensure all team members' voices are heard in decision-making?" Reflect on any mismatches, remembering that no one is perfect and employees are very forgiving when their leaders strive to be values-driven. Then consider what factors might be causing any gaps.

Step 5: Create actionable goals. Choose one or two values where your alignment is low. Set small, achievable goals to bridge the gap. Using fairness as an example once again, you might schedule weekly team check-ins or brief individual meetings to invite input from quieter members.

Step 6: Reflect and revise. It is important that you periodically revisit your values and goals. Ask yourself questions like "Am I living in alignment with my values?" and "What adjustments do I need to make?"

_____

_____

_____

_____

_____

_____

By clarifying and acting on your values, you can reduce the many "mini-crises" and external pressures that contribute to emotional exhaustion and burnout, fostering a greater sense of purpose and fulfillment in your role.

If you are interested in working further on developing your leadership values, there are many free online resources available that can be very useful in assisting you.

• *Case Example: Scott's Journey to Resilience*

Scott, a 53-year-old member of the top management team at a multinational manufacturing company, faced chronic burnout, characterized by severe emotional exhaustion and persistent self-doubt about his performance. His days were dominated by thoughts like "I'll never meet these expectations" and he struggled to find joy in his work. He went home from work each day emotionally exhausted, and he knew he was beginning to distance himself from his colleagues and his employees.

Scott was generally proactive and he wanted to do something to stop this before it went too far. Scott started doing ACT exercises to reconnect with his core values. He dug deep and realized that other people's growth and development was fundamental to why he became a leader. He saw that mentorship and fostering team growth were ways of implementing his values. Scott began to delegate tasks he did not have to be involved in and carved out time for one-on-one mentorship sessions that were more fulfilling for both him and his employees, but that he had been postponing or even canceling. By doing so, Scott not only reduced his workload but also re-energized his leadership.

Additionally, DBT-based mindfulness and emotion regulation practices helped Scott pause and observe his thoughts without judgment, reducing his reactivity in stressful situations. All this helped him feel better about his relationships at work. In turn, his team members grew to value and respect him more as a leader.

At the same time, using cognitive restructuring, Scott began to identify and challenge his negative automatic thoughts. One recurring belief, that "I'm not good enough to lead this team," was replaced with a more balanced perspective: "I bring unique strengths, and I'm continuously learning."

After several months of practice, Scott reported feeling more grounded and aligned with his values. He was invigorated and looked forward to going to work each morning, allowing him to lead once again with passion and purpose.

Conclusion

The emotional toll of burnout on leaders can be enormous and affect the quality of their leadership. Practical exercises like values clarification, DTRs, mindfulness, and emotion regulation empower leaders to navigate burnout, reconnect with purpose and, guided by their values, lead ethically. Scott's journey underscores the transformative potential of these tools—a reminder that with the right interventions, early improvement is within reach. If you take action and persist when you start to feel emotionally exhausted, you have the tools and procedures to be able to disrupt the burnout process and prevent negative effects on your leadership.

Chapter 5

Romantic Relationships

A great marriage is not when the "perfect couple" comes together. It is when an imperfect couple learns to enjoy their differences.

—Dave Meurer

Everyone is familiar with romantic relationships. And if Dave Meurer, American humorist and author of *Good Spousekeeping,* is correct—and he surely is—most people are also familiar with romantic relationship *problems.* One study of over 18,000 couples in Norway—a country renowned for its happy citizens—showed that 77.6 percent of the females and 72.1 percent of the males reported being somewhat, moderately, or mostly dissatisfied with their relationships.[70]

Thus, a case can be made that too many people—and remember, leaders are people too—experience unhappy relationships and just do nothing about it. Some leaders may choose not to seek relationship counseling because of the stigma, time, or financial costs involved, or because it takes both partners to agree to go. In addition, people often stay in unhappy relationships—even those characterized by intimate partner violence—because of financial insecurity or fears about what will happen if they leave. And while it is true that happy couples do not tend to get divorced, this does not mean that unhappy couples do! Concerns about children, social stigma, or financial insecurity are often enough to keep people in unhappy relationships.

This is a pity, for two reasons. First, romantic relationships, and romantic relationship satisfaction, matter deeply. Just being in a romantic relationship is associated with longer life expectancy,[71] and relationship satisfaction is associated with personal wellbeing,[72] life satisfaction,[73] and even mortality.[74] Romantic relationships and relationship satisfaction also spill over onto the quality of leadership behaviors. Second, there are many evidence-based techniques that can help individuals and couples address common relationship problems.

Let's start this chapter by having you identify any romantic relationship issues that you have experienced. And then let's go one step further and have you think about how these different relationship issues affected your work, especially your leadership. After all, as Dionisi and Barling (2019) appropriately entitled their article, "What Happens at Home Doesn't Stay at Home."[75]

REFLECTION EXERCISE 5.1
How Do Relationship Problems Affect My Work?

Use the following grid to write down any relationship issues you may have experienced or are now experiencing and identify the impacts on your work life.

Relationship Issue	Impact on Work/Leadership

When we were writing this chapter, we faced somewhat of a dilemma: virtually all of the research on this topic has focused on *marital* dyads, and *marital* functioning, despite social trends toward fewer marriages and more committed relationships. Second, many romantic relationships consist of combinations other than between a heterosexual, cisgendered man and woman; polyamorous relationships exist among more than two individuals; and gay, lesbian, bisexual, transgender, and queer relationships are much more out in the open these days (at least in certain parts of the world). As a result, except when mentioning results of research that specifically focused only on *marital* dyads, we chose to use the term "romantic relationships" to be more inclusive.

Romantic Relationships and Leadership

Might marriage itself affect leadership? Even if marriage and marital satisfaction are good for you personally, does that necessarily mean they are also good for your leadership? Cho and colleagues learned that married individuals are more prosocial; that being married teaches people humility and self-control (inasmuch as they cannot simply retaliate in the face of even small conflicts), and that married individuals have a longer-term perspective on things like financial investments.[76] Based on a large-scale study carried out from 1993 to 2008, firms led by married CEOs had an 8 percent boost in innovation (as evidenced by patent filings and citations); also, these patents were more oriented to the long term and original rather than exploitative in nature. In a separate study, companies led by CEOs going through a divorce significantly underperformed in terms of operating return on assets and adjusted return on assets. These effects were greater when the divorcing couple had children.[77]

Dumas and Stanko looked at CEOs with children to see the effects on their leadership *behaviors* (rather than leadership *effectiveness*).[78] Leaders who have children were rated higher on transformational leadership by their own supervisors. The reason offered was that parents of children identified more with the family and had learned empathy, developmental, and disciplinary skills that carried over to the workplace.

It's not just your relationship status that matters; it is the *quality* of your romantic relationship. Another study demonstrated that relationship *conflict* in the home was indirectly associated with abusive leadership.[79] Why? Relationship conflict resulted in feelings of depression, and feelings of depression lead directly to abusive supervisory behaviors (for more on depression, see chapter 3).

While most psychological research understandably focuses on negative experiences and outcomes—after all, "bad is stronger than good"[80]—what about positive effects of marital satisfaction on leadership quality? One study investigated the effects of specific positive behaviors within the family, such as laughing together, calmly discussing challenging topics such as financial issues, and engaging in interesting activities together, among American managers.[81] Engaging in positive family events at home resulted in higher levels of transformational leadership at work, as well as higher levels of consideration by leaders for their followers. The researchers concluded that this was because positive family events satisfied basic family needs and prosocial motivation, which then spilled over to work.

In all these studies, the researchers investigated overall relationship functioning. But what about the critical role that more discrete relational behaviors, such as sex, play in romantic relationship satisfaction? Leavitt and colleagues concluded that the frequency with which employed people in a romantic relationship had sex was positively associated with their mood the next morning.[82] A good mood in the morning had a significant positive effect on workplace engagement and job satisfaction throughout the day. Also, the effect of the *frequency* of sex on mood was substantial; for each additional time a partner engaged in sex, there was a 5 percent increase in positive mood the next morning. While job satisfaction and work engagement are not direct measures of leadership quality, positive emotions are more important in influencing your leadership quality and effectiveness than either extraversion or neuroticism,[83] justifying the conclusion that the frequency of sex would probably affect leadership quality too.

Given that a significant portion of romantic relationships experience a decline in satisfaction over time,[84] and given how important satisfaction in romantic relationships can be for leadership quality, we are fortunate that a number of evidence-based skills can be used to enhance romantic relationships of all types.

CBT, DBT, and ACT for Romantic Relationships

First, give yourself some credit: leaders are often skilled problem-solvers, equally adept at managing conflicts and inspiring others. Unfortunately, these same abilities do not always translate seamlessly into romantic relationships. High demands, long hours, dealing with interpersonal conflicts in the workplace, and seemingly impossible deadlines, not to mention leading during enormously challenging times such as the COVID pandemic or the sudden imposition of global tariffs in 2025, all contribute to the emotional toll of leadership, which can then spill over to your personal life and strain even the strongest romantic relationships. Fortunately, CBT, DBT, and ACT, as well as additional approaches aimed specifically at couples, offer a treasure trove of techniques that can be used separately or in combination to help you strengthen your romantic relationship, improve intimacy, and enhance relationship satisfaction.

While all these strategies offer an opportunity to redress many of the "bumps in the road" that we all experience in our relationships, they also do much, much more than that! Think about your car. We often pay more attention to maintaining our cars than we do to maintaining our romantic relationships; we regularly send our cars for tune-ups and maintenance checks, even when they are working perfectly. But do we do anything like that for our romantic relationships? The exercises that follow all allow you to both improve and regularly maintain your romantic relationships.

Cognitive Restructuring

By now you should be familiar with a core concept of CBT: thoughts and behaviors influence feelings, and vice versa. It should come as no surprise that cognitive restructuring can be used to help individual partners and couples identify and modify unhelpful thinking patterns and behaviors that contribute to relationship distress. Just as there are lists of common cognitive distortions for individuals, there are also lists of common cognitive distortions in couples. For example, the cognitive distortion of "mind reading" can lead you to assume that your partner understands your needs without you having to explicitly express them. This in turn can impact your communication style and lead to conflict and resentment, which decrease relationship satisfaction.

Table 5.1 **Common Cognitive Distortions in Couples**

Distortion Name	Definition
Arbitrary Inference	Conclusions are drawn in the absence of supporting evidence. For example, your partner arrives home a half-hour late from work and you conclude, "They must be having an affair."
Biased Explanations	This is a suspicious type of thinking that partners can develop during times of distress when they automatically assume that their partner had a negative motive. For example, "They are acting all sweet because they want me to do something that they know I hate to do."
Dichotomous Thinking	Experiences are codified as either black or white, a complete success or total failure. (This is also known as "all-or-nothing thinking.") For example, you solicit your partner's opinion on a hanging a picture in the dining room, your partner questions the placement, and you think to yourself, "I can't do anything right."

Distortion Name	Definition
Labeling and Mislabeling	This happens if our identity is based on imperfections and mistakes made in the past. For example, after making repeated mistakes in meal preparation, you start to believe "I am worthless as a chef," rather than recognizing error as a part of being human.
Magnification and Minimization	A case or circumstance is perceived in greater or lesser light than is appropriate. For example, an angry partner blows their top upon discovering that the checking account is unreconciled and says, "We're financially doomed."
Mind Reading	This is when one partner assumes that they know what the other partner is thinking without asking or being told. Partners in distress can end up ascribing unworthy intentions to each other. For example, "I know what they are thinking; they think that I am stupid."
Overgeneralization	An isolated incident is allowed to represent similar situations everywhere, whether related or unrelated. For example, after being turned down for a romantic evening, you conclude, "I'll always be rejected."
Personalization	You blame yourself for events or situations outside of your control even when there is no clear evidence that you are responsible. For example, you find your partner rearranging an area you've already organized and assume, "My partner is dissatisfied with the way I do things."
Selective Abstractions	Information is taken out of context and certain details are highlighted while other important information is ignored. For example, your partner fails to answer your greeting the first thing in the morning and you think, "They must be angry at me again."
Tunnel Vision	Sometimes partners only see what they want to see or what fits their current state of mind. For example, someone who believes that their partner "does whatever they want anyway" may accuse them of making a choice based purely on selfish reasons.

REFLECTION EXERCISE 5.2
Cognitive Restructuring of Unhelpful Thoughts About Your Partner

Identify the problematic thought(s). Think about a recent relationship disagreement that was distressing and note the thoughts you experienced before, during, and after it (for example, "I don't have time for this," "This is not going to end well," or "My partner doesn't appreciate me").

Before

_____

_____

During

_____

_____

After

_____

_____

_____

Challenge the unhelpful thought. Look for cognitive distortions that may apply (see Table 5.1). Examine the evidence for and against the thought. Generate alternatives. Could anything else (perhaps unrealistic expectations or miscommunications) be a factor?

Dysfunctional thought(s)

_____

_____

Cognitive distortion(s)

_____

_____

Evidence for and against the thought

_____

_____

Alternative thought(s)

_____

_____

Reframe the thought into a more balanced perspective (for example, "My partner appreciates me but doesn't always express it in the way I expect. If I widen my lens, I can see many signs that I am in fact appreciated").

_____

_____

_____

Commit to behavioral change. List some actions that you can do to reinforce your new perspective, such as verbal affirmations or small acts of kindness and gratitude.

_____

_____

_____

_____

Never underestimate the effects of small acts of kindness and gratitude. These effects, and the ripple effects they have on others and on you, are so profound that this phenomenon is often referred to as "the butterfly effect."[85] As an example, former CEO of Campbell Soup Doug Conant was famous for writing handwritten notes to employees anywhere in the world if they did something special. Imagine the number of employees who felt seen, stayed with the company, rose through the ranks, and became wonderful leaders themselves. Two minutes per note, and the impact across the organization lasts for years.

By its very nature, cognitive restructuring is an activity you will likely need to initiate by yourself. But romantic relationships do not occur in isolation, and the next four techniques are all exercises you would do with your partner. We would also remind you that couples therapy is often indicated for romantic relationship problems—and that books and programs exist to support healthy relationships before any problems may arise.

The DEAR MAN Skill: Assertive Communication

DEAR MAN is an acronym for **D**escribe, **E**xpress, **A**ssert, **R**einforce, **M**indful, **A**ppear confident, **N**egotiate." It refers to a set of assertive communication skills taken from DBT. The rationale for DEAR MAN activities is that communicating more openly, honestly, and respectfully with your partner will allow the two of you to address any issues in a more productive manner. In addition, by clearly expressing your needs and concerns, you and your partner can work toward resolving conflicts more constructively and become more effective at setting healthy boundaries within your relationship, which in turn should enhance relationship satisfaction.

For example, when asserting your needs, avoid saying, "You never prioritize our relationship." Instead, use DEAR MAN to say, "When we don't spend time together, I feel disconnected. I would really appreciate it if we could schedule a weekly date night, as it would help me feel much closer to you and give us an opportunity to check in with one another."

When first learning DEAR MAN, it can be helpful to invite your partner and focus on a relationship issue important to both of you. Share the logic and steps involved in the DEAR MAN activity before starting the discussion.

REFLECTION EXERCISE 5.3
The DEAR MAN Activity

Describe the situation factually, without judgment. What is the situation?

_____

_____

Express how you feel about the situation; explain how it impacts you.

_____

_____

Assert your wants or needs clearly, using "I" statements (this is neither the time nor the place for "you" statements). What do you want or need?

_____

_____

Reinforce your partner if they respond well. Smile and say thank you. Explain why this matters to you and the positive outcomes for both of you that could result.

_____

_____

(Stay) Mindful by keeping your focus on what you want and avoid getting distracted or side-tracked by other issues. List the mindfulness skill you will use (for example: remind yourself of the goal, observe your thoughts and feelings without judgment, pause before responding.

_____

_____

Appear confident by using body language (good eye contact, posture, steady voice) to show confidence, even if you feel nervous or uncertain inside.

_____

_____

Negotiate by being open to a compromise that works for both of you. Think beforehand about what you really want and be willing to negotiate with your partner to get it.

_____

_____

Values-Based Commitment to Your Relationship

Another crucial step you can take with your partner in addressing relationship problems and enhancing relationship (and family) satisfaction is to openly discuss and identify the core values that are most important to each of you in the relationship. Then you can come to a shared understanding of which values you want to prioritize. (Note: this is not about listing the qualities each of you desire in the other!) Derived from ACT, the technique of identifying relationship values is meant to guide the concrete actions that each of you can take—and are willing to commit to—that you believe will actively contribute to enhancing or maintaining your relationship satisfaction. For example, your shared relationship values may include empathy and compassion (understanding and sharing your partner's perspective and emotions), honesty and openness (being truthful and transparent with each other, even with difficult information), and joint decision-making (making choices together). Based on this, you may decide to schedule regular check-ins with one another to hear how each other's days went, communicate any needs or wants (see DEAR MAN), and share decision-making.

Here is how to do it:

1. Set aside some time with your partner to identify your shared values through an open discussion. If either of you gets stuck doing this, it can be helpful for you both to visualize your ideal relationship by closing your eyes and picturing a scenario where the two of you are deeply connected, feeling completely comfortable and loved in each other's presence. You can then distill values from this exercise and actively incorporate them into your daily interactions.

2. Jointly list your top five relationship values and prioritize them.

3. Identify one small action you can commit to doing each day that is aligned with these values that your partner will appreciate.

4. Observe and recognize how these actions impact your relationship satisfaction over time. You can use the following chart to track this information.

REFLECTION EXERCISE 5.4
Values-Based Commitment to Your Relationship

Relationship Value	Committed Action	Accomplished?	Impact on Relationship
1.			
2.			
3.			
4.			
5.			

Bonus: Augment with Mindfulness

Elsewhere we have discussed the many benefits of mindfulness. Consider practicing mindfulness to become more open and aware of how your thoughts, feelings, and actions are moving you either toward or away from the relationship values you have identified, which will allow you to make any necessary adjustments.

Finally, remember that not every moment in your relationship will align perfectly with your individual or shared values. But if you recognize that commitment is a dynamic process, you might find it a little easier to realign your actions with your values even when one of you is knocked off course while navigating the inevitable challenges and stresses that arise in our lives.

"Love Bank" Deposits

Enhancing relationship satisfaction is not just about reducing problems in your romantic relationships; equally important is increasing positive behaviors. The "Love Bank" is a metaphor for how we track how our partners treat us. Just like a financial bank account, we can make deposits and withdrawals from the Love Bank all the time. "Love units" are deposited when we associate our partners with good feelings, and love units are withdrawn when we associate our partners with bad feelings. Our emotional reactions to our partners are determined by the current balance in our Love Bank account. Thus, partners with positive balances are seen as emotionally attractive, while partners with negative balances might not be. By making deposits we are able to increase the amount of love and trust in our romantic relationship and build even healthier relationships over time.

REFLECTION EXERCISE 5.5
Building a Healthy Love Bank Balance

1. Set aside some time with your partner for each of you to list at least five behaviors that make you feel loved.

2. Commit to making at least one "deposit" daily by engaging in an action from your partner's list.

3. Observe and recognize how these actions impact your relationship over time.

You can use the following chart to monitor how your Love Bank balance is doing.

Top Five Behaviors I Will Do to Make My Partner Feel Loved	Top Five Behaviors My Partner Can Do That Would Make Me Feel Loved	Committed Action	Accomplished?	Impact on Relationship
1.	1.			
2.	2.			
3.	3.			
4.	4.			
5.	5.			

If your Love Bank seems quite depleted, it may be helpful to focus on "microbehaviors" you can perform for one another. Microbehaviors are the tiny things that partners do for one another, often when they first meet and are falling in love. Examples include expressing gratitude, showing appreciation, paying compliments, giving affection, and of course, small "random acts of kindness and senseless acts of beauty."

Another reminder: even if you are immediately successful at doing this, it is important to note and accept that conflicts inevitably arise in all relationships, no matter how strong. Negative actions and neglect of any kind by either partner are considered withdrawals that can deplete the account over time, leading to a weaker relationship. Therefore, anytime a withdrawal occurs, it is important for both partners to communicate openly and work to resolve the conflict as quickly as possible. One way to do this is to implement a structured apology approach in which the partner who made the withdrawal acknowledges the harm done, expresses understanding, and makes a commitment to change, thereby building a positive balance before withdrawals further deplete the account.

The 5:1 Ratio

Similar to the Love Bank exercise, the 5:1 Ratio is based on the finding that couples with the most positive interactions ("turning toward" their partner) relative to negative interactions ("turning away" from their partner) were the happiest and had the most enduring relationships. A ratio of five positive interactions to one negative interaction appears to be the magic ratio necessary to help couples balance their Emotional Bank Account and maintain a healthy relationship. Like the Love Bank metaphor, the Emotional Bank Account metaphor posits that to be satisfied in a relationship, couples must focus on increasing deposits (positive interactions) and minimizing withdrawals (negative interactions).

However, the difference here is what must be done during conflicts. During a conflict, the goal is to have 5 positive interactions to every 1 negative interaction; during everyday life, the goal is to have 20 positive interactions to every 1 negative interaction. Why the difference? The 20:1 ratio highlights the importance of building a strong foundation so the couple can better weather challenges when they arise.

Is it fair to have to deposit more than you can withdraw? Perhaps not, but as noted earlier in this chapter, psychologists[86] and relationship experts[87] have long known that "bad is stronger than good." In other words, we remember negative experiences more than positive ones, and negative interactions affect us more than do positive ones. As a result, it takes more positive deposits to develop a positive balance, but that will be well worth the effort—at home and in the workplace.

Here is how to do it:

1. Set aside some time with your partner in which to discuss and commit to say or do five positive things during an argument. For example, you can turn toward your

partner, listen to them, ask them to tell you more, validate their perspective, and express empathy.

2. The next time you find yourself in conflict with your partner, start by reframing your historical approach (for example, "We don't necessarily have to be agreeable or overly accommodating") and remind yourself that you can still do these five things during a conflictive discussion, even if you disagree with your partner and find this issue to be recurring or unsolvable.

3. Track this ratio during any conflicts and note any improvements in your relationship satisfaction.

4. Create a "Ritual of Connection," a small daily ritual that strengthens your bond, such as a morning check-in or a bedtime gratitude practice.

The goal is to cultivate an "emotionally wealthy" relationship through daily routines consisting of positive interactions that can be small, rather than occasional grand gestures such as purchasing an expensive gift or booking a major vacation. In fact, for many couples that have been experiencing problems, just recognizing and acknowledging that they should not take their everyday interactions for granted can make an enormous difference in their relationship satisfaction.

• *Case Example: Leadership, Romantic Relationships, and Reconnection*

Alec and Lata, both in their 50s, have been together for over 20 years. Lata has been the CEO of a small legal firm for 2 years; Alec has worked with the same packaged-goods organization for almost 10 years as a marketing analyst. Lata's organization has been experiencing considerable challenges and she is now working 70-hour weeks, leaving Alec feeling emotionally neglected.

Arguments often ended in defensiveness by both Lata and Alec, and over time, their intimacy dwindled. Both started to have unhelpful thoughts, loaded with cognitive distortions, about why their partners was behaving the way they were. Fortunately, they recognized what they were doing and agreed to work together to improve their relationship satisfaction and intimacy.

They started by using cognitive restructuring to challenge the negative assumptions they were making about each other, replacing them with much more accurate, balanced, evidence-based realities. They then revisited their individual and relationship values and deliberately refocused their time and attention on these, in some small way, each day. In addition, they committed to increasing their daily positive interactions (including using DEAR MAN to communicate around difficult issues) and to return to doing more of the small things for one another that they used to do when they first met, but seemed to have dropped off over time. As they had expected, doing all this took several months of consistent work. In time they learned to reframe conflicts, prioritize their relationship, and rebuild their connection—which led to improved intimacy and greater relationship satisfaction.

Finally, in order to maintain their improved relationship, they implemented weekly "state of the union" conversations and also created a couple's vision statement in which they outlined their long-term goals, values, and commitments to their relationship. This served as a reminder of their mutual aspirations and encouraged ongoing collaboration, which in turn transformed their relationship, improving both their home and work lives.

Conclusion

Romantic relationship problems among leaders are common and, unsurprisingly, often require intentional effort to overcome. By integrating the strategies from this chapter, you can focus on redressing the inevitable challenges that exist (or will inevitably emerge) in your romantic relationship. Even more importantly, you can use many of these techniques to maintain and even enhance the quality of your relationship, creating a ripple effect that will improve both your home and professional lives and make you a better leader.

Chapter 6

Sleep

Innocent sleep. Sleep that soothes away all our worries. Sleep that puts each day to rest. Sleep that relieves the weary laborer and heals hurt minds. Sleep, the main course in life's feast, and the most nourishing.

—William Shakespeare, *Macbeth*

We hear so much about the harmful effects of lack of sleep on leadership behaviors, but how much of a problem is it? The evidence overwhelmingly suggests that we are facing a significant issue.

Simply stated, most people do not sleep enough—and the situation is getting worse. Most experts recommend that you should get *at least* seven hours of sleep each night. In 1975, 7.6 percent of the American population slept for six hours or less.[88] A 2010 study found that slightly over 30 percent of employed people in the United States were sleeping less than seven hours each night. Nine years later, this number had increased to 35.6 percent of the population, and newer studies reveal that 40.5 percent of organizational leaders sleep less than 6 hours per night,[89] while 23 percent of the American population suffers from insomnia.[90]

None of this would be problematic (at least for the scope of this book!) if insufficient or poor-quality sleep did not affect your leadership.

Sleep and Leadership

One study done in Italy showed that supervisors were much more likely to be abusive toward their teams after just one night of poor sleep.[91] Why would poor sleep do this to your leadership? As you no doubt know, having the mental and physical energy to exert self-control and stay focused after a poor night's sleep is a tough ask, especially when confronted by demanding employees.[92]

Barnes also investigated whether insufficient sleep could hurt charismatic leadership. They deprived one group of college students of solid sleep for a night and then asked them to prepare and deliver a 15-minute speech. The sleep-deprived students were rated as significantly less charismatic than those who had slept through the night.[93]

Likewise, sleep-deprived team members were much less likely to notice charismatic leadership behaviors than those who had their usual amount of sleep. If sleep-deprived team members cannot notice charismatic or quality leadership when they see it, they may inadvertently give good leaders lower evaluations. Thus, leaders should not only focus on improving their own sleep but strive to limit after-hours intrusions into their team members' lives that may impact their sleep (such as sending late night work-related emails or text messages).

The effects of sleep on charismatic leadership in all these studies occurred after just *one night* of sleep deprivation, and this was among undergraduate students, who might already be used to sleep deprivation! What about the effects of sleep deprivation night after night among older leaders?

Another study investigated Norwegian naval officers participating in a 14-day combat survival exercise.[94] The officers were deliberately awakened for five consecutive nights and averaged between 2.17 and 2.47 hours of sleep per night. Video recordings indicated that transformational leadership was significantly lower among sleep-deprived officers, who were also more likely to engage in passive leadership.

So, insufficient or poor sleep is common for almost everyone these days, leaders are sensitive to insufficient or poor sleep, and lack of sleep negatively impacts leadership. However, if you are among the many leaders experiencing poor sleep, rest assured (pun intended!) that sleep interventions derived from CBT can make a real difference. A specialized form of CBT adapted for insomnia (CBT-I) improved leaders' job satisfaction, increased prosocial workplace behaviors such as helping work colleagues and self-control, and reduced negative emotions and bullying behaviors.[95]

CBT-I for Better Sleep

There is now overwhelming evidence, dating back to studies in the 1970s,[96] that CBT-I is the most effective non-medication treatment for promoting better sleep.[97] CBT-I can benefit nearly anyone with sleep problems, providing positive results that last with no negative side effects. CBT-I is as effective as the most common sleep medications in the short term and more effective than sleep medications in the long term.[98]

As with mental health problems, different factors such as genetics or aging can predispose people to sleep problems. Like a light switch in the "off" position, however, these predispositions often remain dormant until precipitated by stress, anxiety, worrisome thoughts, or changes in your life that flip the metaphorical light switch on and cause sleep problems. Unfortunately, even if the precipitating factors are resolved, what you think, do, and feel in response to your sleep problems can inadvertently perpetuate them. CBT-I was designed to target perpetuating factors though increased awareness, improved sleep hygiene, cognitive restructuring, stimulus control, sleep restriction, and stress management/relaxation.

Increasing Awareness

How much do you actually know about your sleep? Do you go to bed at the same time each night? How long does it take you to fall asleep? Do you wake during the night? If so, how often and for how long each time? Does anything disturb your sleep? Do you wake up at the same time every morning? Does napping help or hurt?

As with any behavior you want to change, you need to be fully aware of the problem before you can properly address it. You can answer all the above questions (and more) by completing a sleep log. There are numerous versions of sleep logs available; you can use old-fashioned pen-and-paper or modern smartphone apps. While they do not all ask the same questions, they typically ask questions similar to those above. Many also ask about lifestyle factors, such as whether you consumed alcohol or caffeine, took any medications, or exercised during the day.

Which sleep log is the best? The one that you complete fully and accurately every day, ideally for two weeks! One good place to start would be to download the Sleep Diary from the National Sleep Foundation (available at https://www.thensf.org/nsf-sleep-diary). This brief online document is free, easy to understand, takes just a few minutes to complete, and has monitoring sheets for each morning and evening for two weeks. If you prefer something more modern, CBT-I Coach (https://www.ptsd.va.gov/appvid/mobile/cbticoach_app_public.asp) is a free mobile app that can guide you through developing and maintaining good sleep habits.

Keep your sleep log near you and provide as much information as you can before you go to bed and when you wake up. After two weeks, you will have enough data to review and search for patterns. For example, did you sleep better on days you skipped your afternoon coffee? Did a midday nap delay your ability to fall asleep that night? You may also notice that certain lifestyle habits and/or sleep environment issues impact the quantity and quality of your sleep.

Once you have a better idea of the factors that can negatively impact your sleep, you can get to work on changing them. The easiest place to start is by improving your sleep hygiene.

Improving Sleep Hygiene

Sometimes the answer is right in front of us—and so obvious that we miss it! Sleep hygiene involves modifying lifestyle habits and bedroom factors to promote better sleep quality.

Some of the key elements include:

- Create a comfortable sleep environment.

- Avoid caffeine and nicotine close to bedtime.

- Engage in regular physical activity—but not too close to bedtime.

The following exercise will help you reflect on your bedroom environment and how it might be impacting your sleep.

REFLECTION EXERCISE 6.1
Sleep Hygiene: Bedroom Environment Checklist

Description	Yes/No	Plan
Is your bedroom as dark as possible?		
Is your bedroom as quiet as possible?		
Is your bedroom as cool as possible?		
Is your body at the ideal temperature for sleep?		
Is your mattress as comfortable as possible?		

If you answered "no" to any of the above, make a plan to address the problem. For example, if the bedroom is not dark enough, light-blocking shades could be installed, or you could try using a sleep mask. If the bedroom is not quiet, you could install carpeting if noise comes from footsteps on flooring or close windows if noise comes from outside. If the source of the noise cannot be addressed, you could purchase soft foam earplugs or silicone noise canceling earplugs, or use apps that create white, brown, or green noise to mask these sounds.

Your bedroom should not be too warm or cold during the night. Most guidelines suggest keeping the temperature between 60° and 67° F (15.6° to 19.5°C). Similarly, *you* should not be either too warm or cold before going to sleep, which is why you should not exercise too close to your bedtime.

Lifestyle habits can also hurt your sleep. The next exercise asks five questions to assess your daily routine.

REFLECTION EXERCISE 6.2
Sleep Hygiene: Lifestyle Habits Checklist

Factor	Yes/No	Plan
Exercising close to bedtime		
Consuming caffeine in the hours before bed		
Smoking or vaping nicotine in the hours before bed		
Consuming alcohol in the hours before bed		
Using a recreational drug in the hours before bed		
Going to bed very hungry or very full		

If you answered "yes" to any of the above lifestyle habits, develop a plan to address the issue.

While people who exercise regularly tend to fall asleep and stay asleep more easily and generally enjoy better sleep than those who do not, *when* you exercise matters! Exercise in the late afternoon or early evening helps you fall asleep more easily than morning exercise or exercise shortly before you go to bed. If you're experiencing sleep problems, refrain from engaging in vigorous exercise one to two hours before bedtime.

You know that caffeine keeps you awake. While alcohol may help you fall asleep more easily (especially if you are anxious), consuming alcohol before bed can lead to frequent waking and poor sleep. Long-term alcohol use can also lead to sleep disorders such as sleep apnea. We hate to break it to you, but all recreational drugs have disruptive effects on sleep, sleep stages, and consequently, next-day alertness.

Feeling too full or too hungry can also disturb your sleep. If you are hungry before going to bed, a light bedtime snack (especially carbohydrates) may help you sleep.

None of this may work overnight (again, pun intended!). The key to success is to assess and then address each factor you suspect is part of the problem. You can use the information from your sleep log to note the results of any changes to your bedroom environment and lifestyle factors. And when it comes to lifestyle changes, remember the old adage: "Little changes make a big difference in the long term."

Cognitive Restructuring

Many people with sleep problems develop dysfunctional beliefs and attitudes about sleep that then interfere with their ability to fall or stay asleep. Cognitive restructuring can help you become aware of unhelpful thoughts, challenge their veracity or usefulness, and then change or modify them into more balanced, accurate and helpful thoughts.

Table 6.1 provides examples of how to do this. There is space at the bottom of the table for you to insert any other unhelpful thoughts you have, along with how you might balance them.

Table 6.1 **Cognitive Restructuring Examples**

Counterproductive Thought	More Balanced/Realistic Thought
"I will never fall asleep."	*"I might not fall asleep immediately, but even if it takes time to fall asleep, I will eventually do so."*
"I need 8 hours of sleep or else I will never be able to function tomorrow."	*"I may be tired tomorrow, but I have been tired before and still accomplished quite a lot."*
"Here we go again."	*"The only moment that matters is this one. Let me focus on what I can do to set myself up for success right now."*
"I just need to try harder."	*"If I pressure myself, it will just backfire. My best bet is to focus on the things that can help me relax and accept whatever comes my way."*
"I dread bedtime; it makes me feel like a failure."	*"Feelings are not facts. I have overcome many other challenges in my life. As long as I persist with these new strategies and techniques, I can and will improve my sleep."*

Counterproductive Thought	More Balanced/Realistic Thought

Remember, thoughts and feelings are connected, so by learning to catch, challenge, and change your thoughts, you can decrease anxiety and arousal associated with your sleep problems. However, like any other skill, this takes practice; these thoughts are called "automatic" because they often occur without us even being fully aware of them.

Stimulus Control

Are you familiar with the story about Pavlov's dog that was conditioned to salivate every time a bell rang? If so, you will understand that if you struggle with sleep, your bed and bedtime can become signals for wakefulness and anxiety rather than sleepiness. By strengthening "bed" as a signal for sleep, you will learn to fall asleep quickly and stay asleep.

The key elements of this skill include:

- Only going to bed sleepy

- Getting out of bed if unable to fall asleep within a reasonable amount of time

- Only using the bed for sleep and sex

- Going to bed and waking up at the same time every day, including weekends

- Avoiding naps during the day

The following exercise will help you examine whether these elements factor into your sleep routine and make a plan to address them.

REFLECTION EXERCISE 6.3
Bedroom Behaviors

Bedroom Behavior	Yes/No	New Routine
Do you lie down to go to sleep only when you are sleepy?		
If you find yourself feeling wide awake in bed, do you get up and go into another room (or at least get out of bed)?		
Do you limit behaviors in the bed or bedroom to sleep or sex (no reading, watching television, eating, internet, email, or worrying in bed)?		
Do you use an alarm to keep a fixed waking time every day, regardless of how much sleep you got during the night?		
Do you avoid taking naps during the day?		

If you answered no to any of these questions, you may be weakening the connection between "bed" and feeling sleepy! New routines can help you start associating your bed and bedroom with sleep again. Just as with sleep hygiene, the key to success is to assess each factor, address any you suspect may be part of the problem, and then be patient. Remember, sleep logs are essential, so if you have not started one yet, start tonight! You can use the information from your sleep log to assess the results of any new routines.

Sleep Restriction

Many people who struggle to get to sleep try to compensate by going to bed earlier, or by waking up and staying in bed later than usual. However, this often does not help with sleep problems, for several reasons:

1. **Sleep Efficiency:** People who struggle with sleep usually have poor sleep efficiency, meaning they spend a lot of time in bed awake. While you may believe that extending your time in bed is the right thing to do, it can actually worsen the problem and ultimately increase your frustration and anxiety around sleep.

2. **Sleep Drive:** Your sleep drive builds up the longer you are awake. Sleeping in or taking naps after a poor night's sleep can reduce your sleep drive, making it harder to fall asleep and stay asleep.

3. **Circadian Rhythms:** Our internal body clocks are set to certain schedules. Going to bed and getting up much earlier or later than your circadian rhythm dictates can result in lying awake because your body is not yet ready to sleep.

4. **Sleep Quality:** Quality of sleep is often more important than quantity. Staying in bed longer can lead to fragmented, poorer sleep, which is less restorative.

The goal of sleep restriction is to limit the amount of time you spend awake in bed compared to the time you are asleep. When you stay awake longer, your sleep drive builds up, and when you then get into bed, you will likely fall asleep faster and stay asleep more easily. As a result, your sleep efficiency will improve, and you will feel more rested when you wake. This will make it easier to get up on time, causing your schedule to be more aligned with your circadian rhythm, which in turn will make you feel less anxious about falling and staying asleep the next time.

Note: while generally safe, sleep restriction can lead to increased daytime sleepiness, which may pose risks for individuals in certain occupations or with specific medical conditions. If this applies to you, discuss it with your doctor before implementing sleep restriction.

Patience is of the essence when implementing sleep restriction. Stick with it, and you will likely start to see progress in just a few days and then continue to improve from week to week.

You can use your sleep log to calculate your sleep efficiency. Just take the average amount of time you spent sleeping each night and divide it by the average amount of time you spent in bed.

$$\text{Sleep efficiency} = \frac{\textit{Average amount of time spent sleeping}}{\textit{Average amount of time spent in bed}} \; x \; 100$$

If you averaged 4 hours of sleep but spent 8 hours in bed, your sleep efficiency would be 4 divided by 8, which equals 50 percent. If, however, you slept an average of 7 hours a night and spent an average of 8 hours in bed, your sleep efficiency would be 7 divided by 8 = 87.5 percent.

As a leader you are likely used to shooting for perfection, but most experts suggest that a sleep efficiency of 85–90 percent is excellent. Table 6.2 presents some guidelines on how to interpret your sleep efficiency score and adjust your bedtime accordingly. In the empty rows, insert your own information from above.

Table 6.2 **Interpreting Your Sleep Efficiency Score**

Your Personal Sleep Efficiency Score	Meaning of Your Score	Adjustment	Recommended Action Based on Your Personal Score
≥ 90 percent	Excellent—you spend most of your time in bed asleep	Increase time in bed	Set your bedtime **15 minutes earlier**
85-90 percent	Your sleep could probably not be better	Maintain current time in bed	Wonderful—no change needed
< 85 percent	Needs some improvement. You need to spend more of your time in bed asleep	Decrease time in bed	Set your bedtime for **15 minutes later**

If you do make changes, wait at least one week and monitor the impact (using your sleep log) before making additional changes to your bedtime routine. Do not adjust by more than 15 minutes each time.

Make sure you wake up at the same time each day—seven days a week! This is the one thing people with sleep problems can control, and doing so does wonders for your sleep drive and circadian rhythms. But what should your wake time be? Answering this involves taking the average of your wake times from your sleep log and adding 15 minutes. Thus, if your average wake time is 7:30, your fixed wake time should be 7:45.

Your initial sleep window (that is, the time you go to bed each night) should be set according to the average amount of time spent sleeping per night over the past two weeks. For example, if your average time spent sleeping per night was 6 hours and the fixed wake time you calculated above was 7:45 am, then your initial sleep window should be 1:45 am for the first week.

Maintain your sleep log, calculate your sleep efficiency at the end of each week, and adjust your bedtime up or down as indicated in Table 6.2. Continue weekly adjustments until your sleep efficiency is between 85 and 90 percent.

As mentioned above, as you start this process, you may feel more fatigued or sleepy than normal. Do not be discouraged—this is perfectly normal. Many people feel that the quality of their sleep increases after a week or two.

A similar procedure called sleep compression uses an incremental approach, decreasing time in bed more slowly compared to the abrupt change of sleep restriction. This may be a better option for people who experience daytime fatigue or who are sensitive to abrupt alterations in their time in bed pattern.

Stress Management and Relaxation

Aside from unhelpful thoughts about sleep, leaders are often kept awake at night worrying about impending decisions or ruminating about how they mistreated someone.[99] The final ingredient in CBT-I is stress management, which involves learning and practicing relaxation techniques to reduce both physiological and cognitive arousal.

Key techniques include:

- **Progressive muscle relaxation:** Tensing and relaxing the major muscle groups

- **Diaphragmatic breathing:** Focusing on slow, deep, belly breaths

- **Guided imagery:** Visualizing calming and peaceful scenes

- **Yoga:** Combining physical postures, breathing exercises, and simple meditation

- **Mindfulness:** Focusing awareness on the present moment, while calmly acknowledging and accepting your feelings, thoughts, and bodily sensations

Free materials are available on the internet that can aid you in learning each of these techniques. These techniques not only reduce anxiety and promote relaxation before bedtime but can also be used if you awaken during the night or in the early morning.

Which technique is best? As with all the other strategies discussed, the optimal relaxation technique is the one that is easiest for you to learn, practice, and use!

REFLECTION EXERCISE 6.4
Checklist for Sleep Hygiene

Which of the techniques listed above have you tried to assist you in getting better sleep? How effective were they? How many times did you practice? Did anything get in the way? Could you do anything to increase its effectiveness or your odds of success in using it? Write down your thoughts here:

_____

_____

_____

_____

_____

Likewise, which of the techniques listed above that you haven't tried yet appeal to you most? Why is that? How and when do you plan to try using them? What could get in the way? What's in it for you if you do try them?

_____

_____

_____

_____

_____

• *Case Example: Applying CBT for Sleep Problems*

Rachel, a 54-year-old CEO of a multinational logistics company, has had trouble sleeping for several months. She finds it difficult to fall asleep and wakes up repeatedly during the night. She worries about work, as well as her ability to function the next day after a poor night's sleep. After repeatedly trying things on her own and only seeing her sleep problems worsen, she turned to the techniques of CBT-I.

Rachel completed a questionnaire to evaluate the severity of her sleep problems as well as a two-week sleep log to learn more about her sleep patterns. Rachel learned that her average total sleep time was approximately 5 hours, despite the fact that she was spending nearly 8 hours in bed—a sleep efficiency of only 62.5 percent!

Rachel first addressed her sleep hygiene. Having read about the factors that are harmful or conducive to sleep, she decided to limit her caffeine intake and started taking an exercise class during lunch.

Rachel then committed to using her bed only for sleep and sex, and to leaving the bedroom if she was unable to fall asleep within 20 minutes of going to bed. This helped her begin to associate her bed and bedroom with feelings of sleepiness and relaxation rather than wakefulness and anxiety.

After learning that her sleep efficiency was 62.5 percent, she initially restricted her time in bed to 5.5 hours. She set her alarm for 6:00 a.m., resulting in a bedtime at 12:30 a.m.. Over the next four weeks, as her sleep efficiency improved, Rachel increased her time in bed by 15 minutes per week, giving her an extra hour in bed a month later, improving how rested she felt when she awakened each morning, while maintaining an excellent sleep efficiency.

Rachel also realized that her worries at night were interfering with her sleep, so she added cognitive restructuring to her toolbox. Rachel monitored her thoughts and attitudes about sleep and worked on challenging and changing them. With time and practice she learned to replace unhelpful thoughts like "I'll never fall asleep" with more balanced ones, such as "I might not fall asleep immediately, but I will eventually." Rachel also learned to address her work-related worries in the same manner and noticed her confidence rising.

Being an executive is stressful under the best of circumstances, so Rachel decided to learn relaxation techniques. She practiced progressive muscle relaxation in the morning and deep breathing before bedtime, both of which helped reduce her overall levels of stress and physiological arousal. She also took up yoga and added mindfulness to assist herself in letting go of counterproductive thoughts and emotions.

After using CBT-I techniques for just eight weeks, Rachel experienced significant improvement in her sleep. Her sleep efficiency increased, she felt more rested and alert during the day, and she was more focused and less stressed in general. This in turn led to less irritability and better decision-making in her leadership role. Her team noticed this and responded favorably.

Conclusion

Inadequate sleep can hurt your leadership. Fortunately, CBT-I is an effective short-term treatment for insomnia and related sleep problems. You may be interested in using CBT-I yourself and also promoting CBT-I as a tool for improving the wellbeing and productivity of your team. After all, sleep problems can have a significant impact on their mental health and job performance as well. Emphasize the importance of sleep to your team and encourage them to prioritize improving the quality and quantity of their sleep. More importantly, become a role model by limiting workplace intrusions into your team members' lives outside of the workday!

Chapter 7

Substance Use

The first drink may open doors, but the second can close them at work.

—Unknown

The way many people talk about substance use at work, and the procedures that some organizations put in place to regulate against substance use, must surely mean that this is a huge problem for organizations. Is this the case? Substance use scholar Mike Frone's research on the actual prevalence of substance use at work is replacing widespread myths with actual data.[100]

Frone differentiates between substance use among the workforce in general and on-the-job substance use, which he defines as in the two hours before work starts and any time during the workday, including lunch. Another way to think of it is substance use *by* workers versus substance use *at work*. This differentiation is critical: Off-the-job substance use might influence attendance behaviors such as tardiness or absenteeism, while on-the-job substance use may influence job and interpersonal performance, safety, and injuries.[101]

In addition, the differences between recreational drug use among the workforce versus on-the-job use in Frone's large, representative sample of Americans are striking (see Table 7.1). Far fewer people use drugs at work than in general.[102] The data reveal just how few people engage in drug use on the job—especially among people who reported using cocaine or crack cocaine. In addition, more than 90 percent of adults reported that they never used alcohol while at work.

Table 7.1 **Prevalence of Drug Use in the US Workforce and Workplace**[a]

Drug	Use in the Workforce		Use in the Workplace	
	Never	**Overall Prevalence**[c]	**Never**	**Overall Prevalence**
Marijuana	88.67 percent	11.33 percent	98.38 percent	1.62 percent
Cocaine (or crack cocaine)	99.87 percent	1.01 percent	99.87 percent	0.13 percent
Psychotherapeutic drugs[b]	95.10 percent	4.90 percent	98.20 percent	1.80 percent

a   Data taken from Frone (2006a, 2006b).

b   Psychotherapeutic drugs include sedatives, tranquilizers, stimulants, or analgesics used without a prescription, or not in accordance with the prescription.

c   Actual reported use includes less often than once a month, 1–3 days per month, and up to 1–7 days per week.

These findings are trustworthy. First, these estimates are based on a probability sample of all adults employed in the United States. Second, great care was taken as to how questions were constructed, to ensure that respondents would answer sensitive and personal questions honestly. Third, Frone differentiates between alcohol and drugs, and within the latter, further differentiates between marijuana, prescription drugs, and cocaine.

Unfortunately, Frone does not report on the extent of alcohol use among the workforce at large. However, alcohol use on the job was only 8.10 percent. Moreover, with only two exceptions (entertainment and sales groups), alcohol use at work is higher among *managers* than any other occupational group.[103] This may present a classic "fox and the hen" dilemma: are managers less likely to regulate alcohol use at work if they are among the highest users? This could be problematic as a lack of appropriate regulation creates a permissive culture in which employees believe that substance use at work is acceptable.[104]

Did substance use at work increase during the COVID-19 pandemic? More people worked from home during the pandemic—and some still do, where active surveillance by management is less and access to alcohol and drugs greater.[105] Based on a very large survey of Americans, there were notable increases in alcohol use, especially among heavy drinkers, in the early stages of the pandemic.[106] Illicit substance use also increased.[107] The implication is that at the very time we need leaders to be at their best, external stressors might cause more substance abuse.

Alcohol Consumption and Leadership

In a series of clever and realistic simulations, Streufert and colleagues investigated the effects of actual alcohol consumption on different managerial tasks.[108] Moderate drinkers with at least two years of managerial experience spent one day consuming alcohol, until their blood alcohol levels reached 0.05 or 0.10 percent. Their performance was then measured while they completed managerial simulations. In general, speed and frequency of management actions was impaired at 0.10 percent. However, strategic decision-making, which is arguably more important for actual management effectiveness, started to deteriorate significantly at just 0.05 percent.

In another study, Streufert and colleagues investigated the possible effects of hangovers on managerial effectiveness.[109] When participants' blood alcohol levels had returned to zero but they reported feeling hungover, they engaged in the managerial simulations. Intriguingly, while managers thought their performance was harmed when hungover, their objective scores indicated that a hangover seemed to have no effect on effectiveness.

What about excessive coffee consumption and managerial decision-making?[110] Using the same method, Streufert and colleagues compared managers on a day in which they consumed regular amounts of coffee versus a day in which they consumed 400 mg more caffeine. Given that managers sometimes drink coffee to arouse them (especially if not sleeping well—see chapter 6), it is not surprising that there was a mild increase in response speed to incoming task information. However, this was not without its costs: Some aspects of strategic decision-making, such as making the most of new opportunities, declined significantly.

Byrne and colleagues investigated the effects of alcohol consumption *at work* on leadership behaviors, specifically transformational leadership and abusive supervision.[111] They found that on-the-job alcohol consumption stifled transformational leadership and amplified abusive behaviors.

CBT, DBT, and ACT for Substance Use

If you are struggling to manage your use of substances, integrating evidence-based therapeutic approaches from CBT, DBT, ACT, and a technique called motivational interviewing (MI) into your daily routine can not only help you learn to curb your substance use but also be better equipped to manage the unique stressors and pressures that may be leading you to use substances in the first place.

CBT can help you to recognize the triggers that lead to substance use and develop strategies to address the triggers. DBT can help by providing skills to manage your distress and regulate your emotions. ACT can help you to learn to accept rather than avoid challenging situations in your life and to accept urges and other triggers associated with substance use while committing to actions aligned with your personal values. MI can assist you in overcoming any ambivalence you may have about changing your behavior by exploring why change matters to you, your motivations and reasons to change, what's been getting in the way, and how you can move forward in a way that feels right to you.

The exercises that follow target specific aspects of substance use management, adapted to address the unique challenges and demands of your leadership role.

Awareness Training: Self-Monitoring

If you've been reading this book cover to cover, by now you won't be surprised that the first step in managing substance use is to increase your awareness. You need an honest and accurate understanding of your substance use patterns, including triggers like feelings of stress associated with high-stakes meetings or difficult decisions. It will also help to identify any perpetuating factors, such as the unhelpful belief that substance use is a helpful coping mechanism for reducing stress, improving sleep, and increasing confidence.

Awareness training through self-monitoring involves the following four steps:

1. Over the next two weeks, record any instances where you use (or have a strong urge to use) a substance you are interested in reducing.

2. Note the situation you think triggered the urge.

3. List any emotions you felt at the time and any automatic thoughts that you believe contributed to your urge to use.

4. List the emotions and thoughts you had afterward.

Table 7.2 can help you follow this process. By building the habit of completing this table, you will have a quick and easy-to-read summary of all your episodes to reflect on. You will also be able to look for predicable patterns of triggers and how you think and feel after using the substance in question. You will then be able to generate healthier responses using the techniques that follow.

Table 7.2 Awareness Training/Self-Monitoring Form

1 Situation/ Triggering Event (What happened?)	2 Emotions (How did you feel?)	3 Automatic Thoughts (What was going through your mind?)	4 Behavioral Outcome (How much did you drink/use? If none, how strong was the urge?)	5 Emotional Outcome (How did you feel after?)	6 Cognitive Outcome (What was going through your mind after?)

Self-Management: The 3 As

Once you are aware of your patterns, there are many strategies that can be used to modify or disrupt them. For example, three specific evidence-based behavior change strategies that can be applied to your trigger situations are avoiding triggers, altering triggers, and using alternatives—otherwise known as the 3 As of self-management.

Avoid trigger situations: If it is possible to avoid the trigger situation, do so; you will have stopped the process at its first step. For example, if you are trying to limit your alcohol use, you could recommend an outdoor activity or cafe instead of a bar or restaurant when meeting colleagues after work.

Alter trigger situations: If you cannot avoid the trigger situation, you can try altering it in some way to loosen its association with your substance use. For example, if you are trying to curb your nicotine use and you have a pattern of smoking a cigarette with your morning cup of coffee, you could drink a cup of tea or glass of orange juice instead.

Use an alternative: This strategy can be useful by itself or along with avoiding or altering the trigger situation. For example, instead of having a drink to help you to relax after a stressful situation, use a behavioral alternative such as a relaxation technique or going for a walk or run. You could also generate alternatives to unhelpful thoughts. Instead of thinking, "A drink would really help me to relax right now," try "I can manage my stress using a healthier choice in line with my values, like exercise. I don't need a drink."

Cognitive Restructuring

As Norman Vincent Peale said, "Change your thoughts and you change your world."[112] One excellent way to do this is to practice generating alternatives to unhelpful thoughts that are often associated with the contemplation or use of a substance. And as you've learned through this book, by modifying your problematic thoughts you can reduce unpleasant emotions or urges and increase the likelihood of engaging in more adaptive behaviors. The following chart will help you monitor and restructure your thoughts.

Table 7.3 **Sample Cognitive Restructuring Form**

1. Take your answers from the first three columns of Table 7.2 and copy them into columns 1–3 here.

2. In column 4, generate ways of thinking about the situation differently.

3. Note the emotional outcome of doing this in column 5.

1	2	3	4	5
Situation/ Triggering Event (What happened?)	Emotions (How did you feel?)	Automatic Thoughts (What was going through your mind?)	Alternative Thoughts (How might you have viewed the situation differently?)	Emotional Outcome (How did you feel after?)

Mindfulness: The RAIN Technique

The mindfulness skills of DBT and ACT involve being present and aware of your experiences without judging them and then letting go of them, rather than engaging with them through trying to challenge and change them. Mindfulness can assist you in altering what can often be automatic and impulsive reactions to triggers. Instead of trying to suppress or fight an urge, mindfulness involves learning to observe it with openness and curiosity and without judgment.

One helpful approach is the RAIN technique:

Recognize the urge as it arises. Notice what's happening to you and where it's happening in your body.

Allow the urge to exist. Accept your experience as it is, without acting on it.

Investigate the sensations and emotions it brings up. Explore the entirety of your experience with openness and curiosity.

Nurture yourself by practicing self-compassion.. Remember that cravings are temporary experiences that rise and fall like waves in the ocean and are not reflections of who you are.

Distress Tolerance: TIPP Skills

DBT also offers a set of techniques that can be used to manage overwhelming emotions. TIPP, an acronym for **T**emperature, **I**ntense exercise, **P**aced breathing, and **P**rogressive muscle relaxation, is a set of skills that can help manage urges to use substances. TIPP skills are especially useful in moments of high distress and typically provide immediate relief, making it easier for you to withstand cravings without giving in and ultimately strengthening your ability to tolerate discomfort without resorting to substance use.

Here is how to use the four TIPP skills:

Temperature involves changing your body temperature rapidly—such as splashing cold water on your face or holding an ice pack. This calms the nervous system, as cooler temperatures decrease your heart rate, which can help reduce the intensity of cravings.

Intense exercise targets built-up energy from overwhelming emotions by doing some form of a cardio workout. This expends all that conserved energy and allows your emotions to become more balanced. Intense exercise can be immensely helpful for managing intense urges, and the best part is that you don't need to purchase special equipment or join a gym. Just about *any* activity that increases your cardiac activity and burns off excess energy should work, including jumping jacks, push-ups, jumping rope, or taking a brisk walk (up and down stairs is even better). You can even "dance like no one's watching"!

The goal is to do it for about 10–15 minutes. Don't overdo it! If you've not been active for some time, be sure that your physical health allows it. If in doubt, always consult with your primary care physician first.

Paced breathing reduces physical sensations like increased heart rate, flushed face, and sweating often associated with overwhelming emotions and urges, because slowed breathing slows the heart rate, which promotes relaxation. Try inhaling slowly and deeply through your nose for four seconds, holding your breath for four seconds, and then exhaling through your mouth for four seconds, repeating the cycle for 1–2 minutes.

Progressive muscle relaxation involves tightening and releasing muscle groups to relax muscles in your body that become tense when you experience extreme emotions, intense urges, or stress. You can do this lying down, seated, or even while walking. Start at one end of your body and then work your way up or down. For example, you might start by focusing your attention on the muscles in your neck and shoulders, deliberately tightening them for about 5–10 seconds and then releasing them. You should feel them loosening up as you do this. Next, focus on your upper back. Following this, focus on your arms, your abdominal area, back muscles, and finally, your thighs and calves.

Emotion Regulation

Emotion regulation skills from DBT can be used to help you identify, understand, and manage your emotions more effectively, as intense emotions often serve as triggers for substance use. These skills can be especially helpful during periods of high stress, because learning to accurately label emotions, recognize triggers, and use strategies to decrease or increase emotional responses as needed helps reduce the emotional vulnerability that often fuels the urge to use substances.
Here are three examples of emotion regulation skills:

Opposite Action involves identifying emotions driving the urge (e.g., sadness, anxiety) and engaging in behaviors that counteract them—such as reaching out for support instead of isolating or engaging in a healthy activity instead of using a substance.

Checking the Facts is similar to cognitive restructuring in that it involves challenging distorted thoughts that may be used to justify substance use, such as "I can't handle this without using marijuana" and examining whether your beliefs are true.

PLEASE Skills involve treating Physical iLlnesses in a timely manner, balanced Eating, Avoiding mood-altering substances, balanced Sleep, and getting Exercise.

Cognitive Defusion

Cognitive defusion, a core skill from ACT, is similar to mindfulness in that it can help you learn to notice your thoughts and observe them, rather than be controlled by them. This can be particularly useful during moments of self-doubt, helping to prevent the spirals of negative self-talk that often drive substance use. Instead of getting entangled in cravings or believing thoughts like "I need a drink right now" or "I can't handle this without drinking," cognitive defusion encourages you to see these thoughts as just words and mental events—not absolute truths. This will make it easier to stay committed to your values and make values-based choices aligned with your long-term wellbeing, rather than short-term relief.

Here are just a few of many cognitive defusion techniques:

Labeling involves naming your thought in a way that creates some separation from it. For example, "I'm noticing the thought that I need to have a drink" is different than thinking, "I need to have a drink."

Silly voice entails repeating a negative thought in a silly or exaggerated voice to minimize its power.

Singing involves taking the content of your thought and singing it to the tune of a song (perhaps "Happy Birthday") to lessen its grip on you.

Thank you, mind involves not taking unhelpful thoughts too seriously or struggling with them, by simply acknowledging them and saying "thank you, mind" (often with a sarcastic tone, similar to how you might respond to a someone who is saying something to get a rise out of you).

Selling the thought consists of considering how much money the thought would be worth to you or others if you were to sell it.

Visualizing involves imagining thoughts or urges as passing clouds floating by in the sky and observing them without trying to control them. By recognizing that thoughts and urges come and go like passing clouds, you gain the ability to just let them be.

Take this opportunity to practice cognitive defusion using the following exercise.

REFLECTION EXERCISE 7.1
Cognitive Defusion for
Counterproductive Thoughts

1. Take the automatic thought from Table 7.3 that served as a trigger and place it in the first column

2. Note how intense it feels: 0 = not at all, to 10 = extremely intense.

3. Identify the cognitive defusion technique you will use and try it.

4. Note how intense it then feels, from 0 = not at all, to 10 = extremely intense.

Automatic Thought	Intensity of Thought Before (0-10)	Defusion Technique	Intensity of Thought After (0-10)

Values Clarification and Committed Action Plans

Values clarification can help ground you in what truly matters to you. Instead of focusing on short-term relief that often comes from using substances, this technique encourages you to connect with your deeper values—such as family, health, personal growth, or meaningful relationships—making it easier to resist substance use urges when they arise.

Write down your top five values (for example, integrity, compassion, excellence, accountability, family). Use these values as a compass for decision-making when experiencing an urge to use a substance. For example, remind yourself of the long-term benefits of aligning your actions with your core values by asking yourself, "Will using this substance bring me closer to or farther from the life I want?" or "What action can I take right now that aligns with the leader I want to be?"

You can also create a committed action plan (such as calling a loved one or engaging in a hobby) based on your values. This not only provides meaningful alternatives to substance use, but when you anchor your actions to your values, urges often lose their power. You will then feel increasingly confident in your ability to choose actions that support your long-term goals rather than actions that provide a momentary escape from emotions or urges.

Behavioral Activation

Behavioral activation uses activity scheduling to help you improve your mood by increasing your engagement in enjoyable activities that give you a sense of pleasure or mastery or allow you to explore new interests. Behavioral activation can also deal with urges to use substances, as increased engagement in healthy, substance-free activities will help to fill the void that is left after decreasing or discontinuing substance use.

Follow these three steps:

1. Identify key activities that you believe would energize you and that can serve as alternatives to activities or situations involving substance use.

2. Develop a weekly schedule that gradually replaces substance-related activities with these key value-driven activities. Be sure to include non-work activities that provide fulfillment and stress relief, such as exercise, creative hobbies, and quality time with family—(see PLEASE skills above).

3. Track your mood and energy levels before and after engaging in these activities.

Decisional Balance

Not sure if you're ready to change? This is not unusual, especially when it comes to substance use! Motivational interviewing (MI), which was initially developed specifically for people being treated for substance use problems, is often paired with CBT, DBT, and ACT when people are ambivalent about making a change in their lives in any way.

One of the key components of MI is the decisional balance, which can help increase your awareness of both the benefits and drawbacks of your substance use. Completing the MI exercise often helps people recognize that while substances offer short-term relief, they often conflict with personal and professional values and have long-term costs. If you are feeling ambivalent about your substance use, MI might help increase your motivation and commitment to change, or at the very least help you to make more informed decisions about your substance use. The following exercise can help you identify these pros and cons.

REFLECTION EXERCISE 7.2
Benefits and Drawbacks of Decreasing Substance Use

Using the grid provided below, follow these four steps:

1. In the top left box, list all the short- and long-term benefits of your substance use if you were to maintain it at its current level.

2. In the top right box, list all the short- and long-term drawbacks you associate with your substance use at its current level.

3. In the bottom right box, list all the short- and long-term drawbacks you believe will come from decreasing your substance use.

4. In the bottom left box, list all the short- and long-term benefits you associate with decreasing your substance use.

	Benefits	Drawbacks
Maintaining Current Use		
Decreasing Current Use		

Last, reflect on the balance between all these factors. Consider how each box aligns or conflicts with your core values and long-term leadership goals. If you decide to make a change, it can often be helpful to print out the list from the bottom left box, as these are all the ways in which your life will improve if you make a change. It can also help to think about the ways you can lessen the impact of what you'll be letting go of if you decide to make a change (top right box).

• *Case Example: Art's Journey to Self-Management Recovery*

Art is a mid-level executive in a marketing firm. Art's work environment is characterized by high-pressure deadlines and constant change. Despite a record of success, Art was struggling with stress from rapid organizational changes and increasing responsibilities, while his reliance on caffeine and occasional alcohol use at work were beginning to impair his judgment and interpersonal relationships.

Initially, Art's use of caffeine was a harmless way to maintain energy. However, over time, his caffeine consumption escalated, leading to disrupted sleep and heightened anxiety, and his occasional reliance on alcohol before client events began to spread to other work situations in which he felt anxious or stressed. These behaviors started affecting his judgment and personal relationships with employees.

Art began working with an executive coach skilled in CBT. His first assignment was self-monitoring, which he chose to do using a detailed journal. He recorded the times he reached for caffeine or alcohol, noting the situations, emotions, and thoughts associated with these choices. Art realized that most of his substance use was triggered by high-stress meetings, facing tight deadlines, and self-criticism after receiving critical feedback—real or imagined!

Art started using cognitive restructuring to generate alternatives to the unhelpful thoughts like "I must push myself to the limit, or I will fail" that he identified through journaling. By replacing these thoughts with more balanced alternatives ("Taking breaks and self-care are essential for sustainable success"), he gradually reduced his reliance on caffeine as a coping mechanism driven by problematic thoughts.

To manage his acute anxiety and stress in a healthier way, Art began practicing daily mindfulness and distress tolerance techniques—including TIPP skills—to quickly address and ameliorate moments of high anxiety. For example, before giving a challenging presentation, he would engage in paced breathing exercises, which helped to approach presentations with clarity and composure. Doing so helped him to start reducing his on-the-job alcohol use.

Through the use of ACT techniques, Art clarified and reconnected with his core values— health, balance, and relationships. He then developed a committed action plan with two specific goals by using the "alternative" strategy from the 3 As of self-management. The first was cutting caffeine intake to one cup per day, which he did by substituting herbal tea for coffee the rest of the time, and second, he committed to physical exercise and increasing creative hobbies as substitutes for alcohol consumption.

A pivotal moment in Art's journey came during an MI session with his executive coach, who guided him through the decisional balance exercise. This required Art to compare the benefits and drawbacks of continued versus reduced substance use at work. Through this reflective exercise, he realized that while substances offered temporary stress relief and increased alertness, they ultimately compromised his leadership and caused a misalignment with his core values (especially relationships). This MI session deepened his self-awareness and reinforced his commitment to change, providing additional motivation to adhere to his action plan.

Six months after Art's proactive use of these integrated techniques, he noticed that because he had reduced his reliance on substances, he was more effective at problem-solving in high-pressure situations, he was communicating better with his team, and his loved ones were showing more affection toward him. This motivated him to discontinue using substances at work entirely and to continue to limit his use of substances outside of work.

Art's journey underscores the potential of combining multiple methods not only to mitigate substance use but also to promote enduring personal and professional growth. The MI session in particular served as a catalyst by helping him confront his ambivalence and commit to meaningful change. All this energized Art and enhanced his overall leadership performance.

Conclusion

In the demanding arena of leadership, where the stakes are high, the pace furious, and the pressures unrelenting, the techniques and strategies outlined in this chapter are practical tools for building a leadership style that is compassionate, sustainable, and effective. However, the journey to change is not linear, and setbacks may occur. By continually using MI, practicing the techniques from CBT, DBT, and ACT, and seeking support when necessary, you can build the foundation for higher quality leadership. As you move forward, remember that each small step contributes to a larger transformation—one that has the potential to redefine what it means to lead with integrity and compassion.

Chapter 8

Workaholism

Workaholic leaders are often their own greatest strength and weakness; their obsession with work can inspire others but also alienate them.

—Simon Sinek

Before going any further with a topic as ubiquitous as workaholism, we need to ask a question: what exactly is it? Almost all of us toss the word around as if we have a shared understanding of what it is, and no doubt we could name several family members or colleagues who we are convinced are workaholics (present company excluded, of course). Despite this, the fact that there is no universally agreed definition makes it challenging to study—and to treat.

The term itself is not new. Psychologist Wayne Oates was the first to use "workaholism" in his 1971 book *Confessions of a Workaholic*.[113] Oates described workaholism as "the compulsion or uncontrollable need to work incessantly" and is credited for framing workaholism as a behavioral addiction.

After decades of back-and-forth debate, scholars[114,115] now generally agree that workaholism comprises three interrelated but separate components:

1. An inner compulsion or uncontrollable urge to work that leaves the person feeling anxious and guilty when they cannot do so, coupled with an unwillingness or inability to disengage from work.

2. Excessive cognitive involvement in work; workaholics are preoccupied with work, unable to stop thinking about work even when they are not working.

3. A behavioral involvement in work that is excessive; workaholics spend far more time at work than their non-workaholic counterparts.

If workaholism is indeed akin to an addiction, with its inner compulsions and uncontrollable urges, how prevalent is it in the workplace? Andersen and colleagues' large-scale study on tens of thousands of people in over 20 countries is revealing.[116] They estimated that workaholism affects 14.1 to 15.2 percent of people. However, they do not provide a separate estimate for *leaders*, leaving open the question of whether workaholism among leaders would be higher or lower than the general population. We have our suspicions here though! Is there something about leaders' roles that could make workaholism more likely?

There are compelling reasons to suggest that workaholism is more heavily influenced by workplace factors than personality traits. In one study, for example, police officers' levels of workaholism were tied directly to daily work demands.[117] Only a few personality traits (such as perfectionism, extraversion, type A behavior) are associated with workaholism, while workplace factors such as work overload and conflict, work hours and overtime, commitment to the organization and the time commitment to the job, and job involvement are all associated with higher levels of workaholism. At the same time, Clarke and colleagues showed that just holding a managerial position is positively associated with workaholism.[118] Thus, we are confident that workaholism among leaders would be higher than the general population (more than 15 percent) and only the question of *how much* higher is yet to be answered.

This is concerning, as the negative effects of workaholism cast a very wide shadow on wellbeing. First, workaholism is associated with poorer physical and mental health in general, including problems such as blood pressure and insomnia.[119] Second, leaders' workaholism is associated with employees' psychological distress.[120] Third, given the additional time and emotional commitment that workaholics invest in their work, workaholism exerts a toll on family dissatisfaction and work–life conflict. Moreover, one partner's workaholism indirectly diminishes their partner's relationship satisfaction, highlighting how family members are inevitably swept up in its negative impact (see chapters 5 and 9).[121]

Workaholism and Leadership

Debate continues as to whether workaholism is a double-edged sword, as can be seen from Simon Sinek's statement that opened this chapter. Sinek's presumption is that we should expect positive effects on performance, but negative effects on wellbeing. Yet we could find no direct evidence for positive effects of workaholism on leadership performance. On the contrary, research on workplace performance makes the case that workaholism can be detrimental for leadership.

From their meta-analysis of 12 separate studies involving nearly 7,000 people, Clarke and colleagues saw consistently strong and negative effects on critical performance outcomes such as job satisfaction and job stress, helping behaviors, and all three dimensions of burnout discussed in chapter 4.[122] More recent research in China and the United States demonstrated no benefits of compulsive or excessive work habits on employees' performance.[123]

Ironically, the only positive outcome of workaholism was leaders' career prospects: Higher levels of workaholism were associated with better career prospects. Leaders will need to ask themselves whether the personal and familial costs are worth the exchange.

Because workaholics are compulsively focused on results and just getting work done, they are less focused on more productive challenges of leadership such as mentoring, supporting, networking, and creating opportunities for their employees.[124] A study on police officers showed that the higher their levels of workaholism, *the less likely* they were to voluntarily engage in the kind of behaviors that helped employees or the organization as a whole.[125]

Balducci and colleagues studied a health care service organization in Northern Italy. They found that workaholism was positively associated with bullying, such as ignoring, gossiping about, insulting, criticizing, or shouting at others.[126] If anything, they may have underestimated workaholism and bullying; the researchers asked leaders whether they bullied others, but the workers were not asked whether they were bullied. It's possible that leaders underestimated their bullying to create a positive impression. Bullying behaviors are very similar to what is termed abusive supervision, and a meta-analysis of 130 studies on abusive supervision did not reveal a single positive outcome.[127]

So much for the notion that workaholism is a double-edged sword! The lesson is clear: There are just no benefits of workaholism on leaders' performance and wellbeing—or those of their team members, their own marriages, or their partners. Organizations need to assess their cultures and determine how many of their practices reinforce and reward workaholism.

Leadership development initiatives can be used to reinforce these lessons among leaders themselves. How these initiatives are framed is important: Experience teaches us that when leaders are offered "time management programs," few attend. But when they are offered programs to enhance "time use strategies," far more show up. A key challenge is to prevent leaders from thinking that the goal is to strip them of the very characteristics that they believe helped them be successful in the first instance. (For this unhelpful thought, cognitive restructuring would be especially helpful!)

Fortunately, you do not need to wait for your organization to act, nor for the effects of any such initiatives to take effect. Engaging in some of the activities set out in this chapter can help you start to make changes for yourself, with potentially considerable benefit not just for you but for the other important people in your life as well.

CBT, DBT, and ACT for Workaholism

Practical, evidence-based exercises provide a wide variety of skills that can assist you in breaking free from your workaholic thoughts, actions, and compulsions. The techniques that follow are designed to help you not only rethink and alter your approach to work but also implement tangible behavioral changes that align with your core values. All this can help you foster a more balanced and effective leadership style and lead a happier and healthier life.

Cognitive Restructuring

You know that thoughts play a critical role in influencing both our emotions and actions. You also know that a main challenge of cognitive restructuring is that we are often not aware of our thoughts. For example, when is the last time you thought of all the steps involved in driving your car, instead of just getting in your car and driving it? Cognitive restructuring can help you to become aware of your internal monologue and then gradually modify any unhelpful thought patterns that contribute to your workaholism.

Here are four steps to cognitively restructure your workaholic thoughts (see Table 8.1):

1. Over the next two weeks, maintain a DTR (see chapter 4) to increase your awareness of your automatic thoughts. The key times for recordings are moments when you feel compelled to overwork. Be sure to note the trigger situation, the specific thoughts that come up, and the emotions you feel. If you cannot complete the record at the moment, do it as soon as possible, imagining yourself in the situation to help access what triggered you as well as what you were thinking and feeling at the time.

2. Challenge each unhelpful thought. You can challenge its validity by looking for cognitive distortions and/or by asking questions like: "What evidence supports this belief?" or "Am I magnifying the negatives or ignoring positives?" You can also generate alternatives by asking: "Is there a more balanced or realistic way to view this situation?" You can even challenge its usefulness by asking: "How does it benefit me to think this way?"

3. Replace the unhelpful thought with more constructive alternatives. Be sure to write them down and rehearse them. For instance, you can reframe "I must do everything myself" to "Delegating can enhance team performance and build trust."

4. Use the blank table to challenge your own cognitive distortions.

Table 8.1 Examples of Cognitive Distortions and Constructive Reframes

Trigger Situation	Emotion	Problematic Thoughts	Cognitive Distortions	Questions to Challenge the Belief	Alternative/ Constructive Reframe
Working in bed	Anxious; stressed; guilty	"If I'm not working every minute, I'm failing."	All-or-Nothing Thinking	Is there a more realistic way to view this?	"Balanced effort leads to sustainable success."
Working through lunch	Anxious; fearful; stressed	"Taking a break will result in disaster."	Catastrophizing	Where is the evidence to support this?	"Rest rejuvenates my creativity and decision-making."
Working on subway ride home	Stressed; guilty; anxious	"Every idle moment is wasted time."	Overgeneralization	How does it benefit me to think this way?	"Strategic downtime is essential for peak performance."

Trigger Situation	Emotion	Problematic Thoughts	Cognitive Distortions	Questions to Challenge the Belief	Alternative/ Constructive Reframe

Behavioral Intervention: Developing Coping Mechanisms

Developing healthy coping mechanisms is critical for managing the stress and anxiety associated with trying to break free from workaholism. Relaxation techniques such as deep breathing or progressive muscle relaxation, time management skills, and perhaps toughest for workaholics, setting boundaries can be especially useful when addressing workaholism. These coping mechanisms will provide you with a sustainable way to manage stress, leading to better work–life balance and wellbeing, ultimately making you a better leader.

Deep breathing can slow your heart rate, calm your mind, and create space for you to pause before you compulsively dive back into the very work you're trying to break free from. One well-established, simple method involves slowly inhaling through your nose for four seconds, holding your breath for four seconds, and then exhaling forcefully through your mouth for four seconds, making a "whoosh" sound. Repeat at least three times.

Progressive muscle relaxation involves systematically tensing and relaxing different muscle groups, starting from your head or your toes and working to the other end. (More information on this in chapter 1.)

Time use strategies will help you make better use of your time and energy. Former U.S. President and 5-star General Dwight Eisenhower was known for his incredible ability to prioritize. The quote that "I have two kinds of problems: the urgent and the important. The urgent are not important, and the important are never urgent" led to the development of what is now known as the Eisenhower Matrix. This may be especially relevant and useful for workaholics, as it can help you to distinguish between what is urgent and what is important. Here's how to do this, using the chart on the following page.

1. Start by making a list of everything you have on your plate right now, both work and personal tasks; don't worry about the order.

2. Place all these tasks in the appropriate box, urgent or not urgent.

3. Examine where you are spending most of your time. Is it on tasks from quadrant 1 (the ideal), from quadrants 2 or 3 (less than ideal), or from quadrant 4 (worst possible)?

4. Check off what you can *delegate* from quadrants 2, 3, and 4.

5. Scratch off what you can *eliminate* from quadrant 4.

6. Revisit this matrix over time, with the goal of ensuring that "quadrant 1" activities take up most of your time.

REFLECTION EXERCISE 8.1
The Eisenhower Matrix

	Urgent: Needs Immediate Attention	Not Urgent: Can Be Scheduled for Later
Important: Contributes to Long-Term Goals and Values	Quadrant 1:	Quadrant 2:
Not Important: Little Impact on Long-Term Success	Quadrant 3:	Quadrant 4:

Setting boundaries at work is essential for overcoming workaholism. Take a lesson from famed basketball coach John Wooden, who insisted that "you develop respect by finishing on time." We would add that you also develop respect by starting on time. When you start and finish meetings on time, you respect team members' responsibilities and obligations. Once you have mastered this—and initially, it won't be easy—extend the idea to include what time you start and finish work and respect those boundaries. As you improve this skill, set boundaries for other activities such as lunch, how much time you will spend on emails, and so forth. And be sure to tell your team members about your boundaries; as a mark of respect, they will honor your boundaries too (and you'll be modeling this behavior for them).

Mindfulness

As you will recall, practicing mindfulness allows you to build the skill of observing your thoughts and emotions (including urges) without judgment. Once you are aware of your triggers (see Table 8.1), mindfulness can be a powerful tool to help you recognize when you might be about to slip into overworking.

Start by setting aside a few minutes each day for practice. Find a quiet space where you can sit comfortably, close your eyes, and focus on your breathing. Observe each inhale and exhale without forcing it. If intrusive thoughts about work arise, gently acknowledge them without judging them, then practice letting them go and bringing your attention back to what you are doing in the present moment (in this case, just breathing). Expect your mind to wander frequently, as that's what minds do! The "muscle" being built here is your ability to detach from a troubling thought and redirect your attention to whatever you're doing in the here and now.

Don't like mindful breathing? That's okay; the good news is that you can integrate mindfulness into any aspect of your daily routine—during a meal, brushing your teeth, or riding the subway. What is important is focusing your attention fully on whatever you are doing in the moment and nothing else, incorporating all your senses, and returning your attention to whatever you are doing whenever your mind wanders away from it. While amazingly simple in concept, this is definitely not easy and takes lots of practice and patience. Regardless of how you practice mindfulness, over time it can help you build self-awareness and recalibrate your focus, reduce your stress, and ultimately lead you toward a healthier and more sustainable involvement with work.

Distress Tolerance

Distress tolerance skills from DBT such as the TIPP skills (see chapter 7) can help you manage intense emotions and challenging situations without resorting to counterproductive behaviors such as excessive work. Such skills can be particularly useful for workaholic leaders who are aware when they push themselves (or others) too hard.

The following distress tolerance skills taken from DBT can also help:

Radical acceptance is about accepting things as they are, not as you believe they should be. Radical acceptance can help break your cycle of workaholism by allowing you to acknowledge reality as it is, rather than constantly striving for perfection or the unattainable. The goal is to accept feelings of discomfort that may arise from the decision to work less, without judgment. The cognitive component to radical acceptance involves acknowledging that no matter how much you work, there will always be more work and that your self-worth is not defined by your productivity. By embracing this mindset, you can get better at letting go of the pressure to overwork and make more intentional, values-based decisions about how you prioritize your time, wellbeing, and leadership activities.

STOP skills (Stop, Take a step back, Observe, and Proceed mindfully) provide a structured way of making more conscious decisions about your work habits and resisting the impulsive actions that are often at the core of workaholism. For example, if you feel the urge to check emails during your personal time, you can learn to "stop" by consciously pausing whatever you're doing and acknowledging the need to take a break. "Take a step back" involves mentally disengaging from the trigger situation at work and allowing yourself a moment of reflection and perspective. Next, "observe" what's happening internally and externally—noticing without judgment any thoughts, emotions, and physical sensations driving your urge to overwork. And finally, "proceed mindfully" involves making conscious, values-based choices—taking a break from work, setting a boundary, prioritizing tasks differently, or engaging in a self-care activity. Practicing the STOP skills regularly can help you break automatic work habits.

IMPROVE skills (Imagery, Meaning, Prayer, Relaxation, One thing in the moment, Vacation, Encouragement) provide a structured way to help counter workaholism by shifting your focus from work, fostering balance and resilience. For example, if an uncontrollable urge or impulse to work arises, you can use imagery to visualize a more balanced version of your life. You can then find meaning by reminding yourself why relationships and relaxation matter to you just as much as productivity. Next, you might engage in a prayer or a moment of quiet reflection, and then use relaxation techniques, like deep breathing or stretching, to ease any intense emotions or physical tensions you are experiencing. You may then focus your attention on one thing in the moment, like your breath. If need be, take a brief vacation to allow yourself to reset—even if that means simply stepping outside of the office or turning off the screen(s) for a few minutes. And finally, you can practice encouragement by speaking to yourself with kindness (this can be incredibly challenging if you tend to be self-critical), reminding yourself that you deserve to take a break and that your worth extends beyond your work.

By cultivating these distress tolerance skills, you can create a buffer against the urge to over-work that will allow you to reframe your perspective and accept any unpleasant emotions and sensations that may arise. This in turn will allow you to endure emotional discomfort and reduce the impulse to dive back into work as a coping mechanism, instead finding relief through deliberate focus on value-driven actions and activities.

Values Clarification and Committed Action

Values clarification and committed action skills can also be applied to workaholism. Over time you will learn that the best of leadership is grounded in living a balanced life where professional accomplishments do not have to come at the cost of personal wellbeing, and in fact, are often a result of having invested in your personal wellbeing.

The next exercise can clarify how to live a value-driven life.

REFLECTION EXERCISE 8.2
Values Clarification and Committed Action

1. Clarify your core values by taking time to reflect on what matters most in your life. Consider values such as family, health, personal growth, and community. And yes, you can also include work-related values such as integrity and respect. Ask yourself, "If work weren't my main focus, what would I want my life to be about?"

2. Develop a values-based action plan by listing specific actions that embody each of your core values. For example, if "family" is a core value, set a goal to spend regular quality time with family by making it home in time for dinner at least three nights per week and planning a weekly family outing.

3. Use some of the tools described earlier in this chapter to accept any emotional discomfort that may arise. Understand that as you work toward behavioral change, it is natural to experience feelings such as guilt or anxiety. Instead of succumbing to these feelings or even trying to resist them, use the other skills you have been practicing to simply notice and acknowledge them while reminding yourself of the reasons for your behavioral change.

4. At the end of each week, review your values action plan and assess the extent to which your activities aligned with your values. If necessary, adjust your schedule and priorities. Stay committed to your values action plan by redirecting your efforts whenever you veer off course.

You may wish to create a grid like the sample one provided below.

Table 8.2 **Example Values Action Plan**

Step 1	Step 2	Step 3	Step 4
Top five values	Actions that embody each value	Positive and negative emotions associated with actions	Extent (0–10) to which your activities during the week aligned with each value and reactions to this score
1. *Family*	*Making it home in time for dinner at least three nights per week.*	*Stress and guilt about leaving work "early" when more could be done. Joy of seeing the excitement from my kids when I made it home for dinner.*	*Made it home two nights this week. An opportunity to be gentle with myself and flexible with my standards—and to try again next week!*
2.			
3.			
4.			
5.			

Putting It All Together: Integrating Behavioral Change into Your Daily Routine

Successful change from workaholism to a more balanced leadership style requires a structured approach to develop new, daily habits. Table 8.3 provides a sample daily routine that integrates the practical exercises detailed throughout this chapter, blending cognitive restructuring, emotion regulation, distress tolerance, and mindfulness and acceptance-based strategies with behaviors that align with your core values.

Table 8.3 **Example Daily Routine**

Time of Day	Skill	Purpose
Morning	Mindfulness and Relaxation	Ground yourself, let go of worrisome thoughts, set positive intentions for the day at work and at home
Mid-Morning	Cognitive Restructuring	Identify and reframe any emerging negative automatic thoughts
Lunch	Mindfulness and Relaxation	Recenter, refocus, and reduce stress before resuming work
Afternoon	STOP Skill	Interrupt compulsive work urges during high-pressure moments
Late Afternoon	Values Clarification and Committed Action Plan	Assess alignment of actions with core values each day and consider any adjustments that need to be made
Evening	Relaxation and Committed Action	Disconnect from work, reduce stress, and engage in restorative personal activities

Use this example to make your own plan.

By adopting a structured routine that incorporates cognitive restructuring, mindfulness, values-based actions, and so on, you can gradually rewire your work habits. Over time, this will not only reduce your tendency to overwork but also enhance your overall wellbeing and effectiveness as a leader.

- *Case Example: Sandy's discovery of a healthy lifestyle*

  Sandy, a 45-year-old chief financial officer at a rapidly expanding health care organization, was celebrated for her tireless work ethic and relentless pursuit of excellence. However, this dedication came at a significant cost. Sandy's work habits resulted in late nights at work, compromised sleep, and a gradual erosion of her personal relationships. Recognizing the unsustainable nature of her approach to work, she sought help from a psychologist. Together, they created a structured treatment program with techniques from CBT, DBT, and ACT, with a focus on both cognitive and behavioral change.

Sandy began by maintaining a daily thought record. She discovered that one recurring belief was "If I don't immediately address every work issue myself, I'm letting my team down." With help from her psychologist, she evaluated the evidence for and against this thought and noted times when pausing to brainstorm solutions and delegating to others led to better outcomes. By challenging her all-or-nothing mindset, Sandy reframed her beliefs to be more balanced, such as "Delegating responsibilities empowers team learning, promotes collaboration, and actually gets better results." Over several weeks of reminding herself of this new perspective, she experienced less anxiety when not immediately addressing issues, and she was able to moderate her compulsive work behaviors and comfortably delegate work to others.

As part of her new daily routine, Sandy initiated a 15-minute mindfulness practice each morning. Initially, she struggled with intrusive thoughts about work, but with persistent patience and practice, she became increasingly adept at viewing these thoughts without judgment. She also applied the STOP technique when faced with the urge to check emails incessantly during high-stress periods. During one intense project deadline, she paused to note her physical tension and took a short walk. This brief interruption allowed her to return to work with a clearer, calmer mindset. Over time, such actions reduced many of the obsessive thoughts at the core of her workaholism.

Perhaps the biggest change came when Sandy completed the values clarification exercise. Sandy identified three core values: family, personal growth, and leadership integrity. She then developed a values-based committed action plan, which included scheduling weekly family dinners, setting aside time to practice karate, and establishing a mentorship program within her organization. Although adjusting her schedule to meet these commitments was initially challenging (she felt guilty), Sandy practiced accepting uncomfortable emotions as a natural part of her transition from workaholic to a more balanced life. Over time, her commitment to living according to her three identified core values helped her to reduce her overreliance on work as her sole source of self-worth; she also found it easier to let go of uncomfortable emotions.

Within four months, the results were remarkable. Sandy reported a significant reduction in her weekly working hours as well as significant improvements in her sleep quality. Her renewed sense of purpose and energy did not go unnoticed by her team members and led to enhanced collaboration and creativity, increased engagement, and proactivity. On a personal level, her family relationships also improved markedly, and she experienced a newfound sense of balance and fulfillment, underscoring the idea that success is defined not solely by professional achievements but by a harmonious integration of personal and work life.

Conclusion

The time has come for leaders to stop seeing excessive work as a badge of honor, bragging about how much they work and how stressed they feel. People who "stress brag" are seen as less competent and compassionate by others, receive less help from their peers, and through the process of emotional contagion,[128] create more stress and burnout for their coworkers.[129] Workaholism has many personal, familial, and work-related costs with few if any benefits. Remember: the essence of leadership lies not just in what you achieve at work but also in how you live and inspire others to enjoy fulfilling lives themselves. By scheduling your priorities and committing to both cognitive and behavioral change, you pave the way for a legacy of wellbeing, creativity, and lasting impact.

Chapter 9

Work–Life Balance

There's no such thing as work–life balance…There are work–life choices, and you make them, and they have consequences.

—Jack Welch, CEO of General Electric

We have come a very long way since Jack Welch, a controversial business leader remembered both as "the ultimate manager" and "the CEO of the century," but also as "neutron Jack" and "Jack the ripper," patronizingly offered this advice to mothers.[130] What we now know is that advice like that is simplistic, misguided, and misogynistic. Work–life balance is not just a binary choice about how you choose to divide your time each day; rather, work–life balance directly and indirectly affects your wellbeing[131] and personal, family, and work relationships.[132]

It affects the quality of your leadership too.

Work–Family Balance and Leadership

Within the broad area of work–life balance, the conflict between work and family has attracted the most attention; it has been widely studied for at least the past 50 years. The multiplicity of demands that leaders face at work and how they cope with their leadership roles may well affect what happens at home—and vice versa. Actively dealing with simultaneous but contradictory demands of work and family can be incredibly stressful and overwhelming, even for the most capable of leaders.

But can we say with certainty that work–family conflict affects the quality of leadership? Fortunately, there are some good studies that provide a balanced and nuanced answer to this vexing question.

Work–Family Conflict

Coping with competing work and family roles and responsibilities can leave you emotionally drained—leading to increased impatience and irritability, which are likely to affect your responses. Most research has framed this question in terms of conflict between our work and family *roles*, with the expectation that experiencing conflict between these roles would negatively affect leadership quality.

We saw in chapter 5 that depression amplifies the effects of marital relationship conflict on abusive supervision. Leaders who experience problems with balancing work and family roles and responsibilities tend to become more distracted and less able to concentrate when they are working. This hindered their ability to devote time and energy to routine leadership tasks such as appropriately praising or punishing employees.[133]

What can be done to ameliorate work-family conflicts and their effect on leadership performance? Fortunately, positive family and non-work experiences can have positive effects on leadership quality.

Family-Work Enrichment

McClean and colleagues turned their attention to the indirect effects of *family-work enrichment* (FWE) in the United States.[134] Confirming the notion that events and feelings in one domain of our life spill over in to others, positive events at home can leave you feeling like you have the energy and confidence to overcome challenges at work, including enacting quality leadership. (FWE was reflected by questions such as "The love and respect [I] get at home makes [me] feel confident about [my]self at work,"[135] and "Since work yesterday, my family has made me feel happy and this helped me be a better worker.")[136] FWE indirectly and positively affected transformational leadership. Magnifying the lesson that we cannot ignore the role of our home lives, these positive effects were stronger for leaders whose early upbringing had left them with secure attitudes toward relationships.

Backing this up, Lin and colleagues conducted two studies on FWE and leadership behaviors.[137] FWE indirectly enhanced transformational leadership and good management behaviors. FWE left leaders feeling satisfied with their home lives and wanting to make a difference in their team members' lives, which in turn resulted in better leadership and management behaviors. The benefits were even stronger for leaders who had children and who generally felt that family life was important.

There is every reason to believe that balancing our personal activities, hobbies, volunteering, and home life responsibilities with our work responsibilities can have positive consequences on leadership quality. If you have been struggling with balancing either your work and family responsibilities or your work and personal life, the good news is that there are many evidence-based techniques that offer practical strategies for regaining your balance. Let's turn to a few of these now.

CBT, DBT, and ACT for Life Balance

Achieving life balance is challenging for so many people these days, with increased responsibilities, longer working hours, and technological demands blurring work and personal boundaries. For leaders, we can add to this the immense stress and pressure associated with the constant attention and transparency of being in high-level positions. With this in mind, we now provide actionable techniques and exercises derived from CBT, DBT, and ACT to optimize the balance between your work and personal lives.

Cognitive Restructuring

As we've mentioned throughout this book, cognitive restructuring can help you identify, challenge, and change problematic thoughts to create emotional relief and more healthy and productive behaviors. In the case of work–life balance, leaders often experience automatic thoughts such as "Taking time for myself is a sign of weakness (or even selfishness)" or "I can't afford to prioritize my family over work." Hopefully, you now recognize the cognitive distortions in these thoughts that drive pressure and urges to overwork—often at the cost of those around you and, ironically, productivity.

Here's how to go about it:

1. Engage in self-monitoring for 1–2 weeks, paying particular attention to specific situations when thoughts arise that undermine your work–life balance.

2. Identify a recent situation where you felt overwhelmed by work–life demands.

3. Write down the automatic thoughts you had about yourself or the situation.

4. Practice challenging the thought using a variety of questions, such as "Is this thought helping or hindering my wellbeing?" or "Is this thought based on fact or assumption?" or even "What would I tell a colleague in my position?"

5. Write more balanced and realistic alternative thoughts, such as "Prioritizing rest enhances my performance" or "Setting work boundaries allows me to lead more effectively."

Use the following grid to write down your ideas, following the example we give in the first row.

REFLECTION EXERCISE 9.1
Practicing Cognitive Restructuring for Work-Life Balance

Situation	Automatic Thoughts	Question(s) to Challenge the Thought	More Balanced and Realistic Thought
Missing my child's performance due to work obligations.	*"I'm failing as a parent."*	*"What would I tell a colleague in my position?"*	*"It sucks that you missed that one. You can't be everywhere all the time, but you can begin to make quality time with your family a priority."*

Consistently practicing cognitive restructuring can enable you to feel less stress or guilt when choosing to create a healthier work–life balance and approach the professional demands on your life with greater flexibility and perspective. Doing this also fosters enhanced leadership and personal fulfillment.

Behavioral Activation

Behavioral activation can improve your work–life balance by helping you intentionally schedule enjoyable and meaningful activities into your workweek. Leaders often become consumed by professional demands, sacrificing personal activities that bring them joy, connection, and rest— and in so doing, paradoxically contribute to their feelings of burnout and diminished wellbeing. Behavioral activation reverses this cycle through the purposeful planning of pleasurable and values-driven activities to restore balance.

A great place to start is by identifying activities that you previously engaged in that brought you a sense of joy or connection, such as exercising or spending time with family or friends. You might also identify activities that you currently engage in that could be ramped up. Finally, you can identify activities that you've never tried but think would bring you a sense of meaning or balance, perhaps like learning to play an instrument.

The next step involves creating a weekly schedule that treats these activities with the same priority as work commitments. If you find that your motivation is low—initially or at any time in the process—then you can start with the decisional balance exercise described in chapter 7 or the cognitive restructuring exercise described above to challenge any unhelpful thoughts, such as "I don't have time for this" or "This isn't productive." Then restructure those thoughts into more helpful and motivating thoughts, such as "Prioritizing relationships fuels my leadership capacity." Over time, if you persistently make time for enjoyable and meaningful activities in your week, you should begin to experience enhanced mood, reduced stress, and a renewed sense of energy— all of which can reinforce the steps you've taken and contribute to greater resilience and enhanced leadership.

The next exercise can help you incorporate new activities into your life.

REFLECTION EXERCISE 9.2
Planning Pleasurable and Meaningful Activities

1. Brainstorm as many activities as you can in the Joy/Pleasure and Meaning/Mastery columns, paying particular attention to activities that foster connection to people in your personal life. It's okay (and in fact, better!) if some activities fall in both columns.

2. Schedule at least one activity from the Joy/Pleasure and Meaning/Mastery columns in the Schedule Date/Time column.

3. Track your mood, stress, and energy before and after each activity.

Joy/Pleasure	Meaning/ Mastery	Schedule Date/Time	Mood, Stress, Energy Before	Mood, Stress, Energy After

Mindfulness

Mindfulness can help you achieve greater work–life balance by increasing your emotional awareness, which in turn can reduce reactive decision-making. Leaders often experience intense emotions like anxiety, guilt, and frustration over their work demands, which can compel them to react by overworking. Lack of good boundaries can lead to sacrificing personal time for even more work.

You'll note that, as with cognitive restructuring, we've suggested mindfulness as a tool in many other chapters in this book. That's because it works! Mindfulness can enhance your emotional awareness and increase clarity in your decision-making, which in turn should reinforce healthier work–life boundaries. And remember: the more you practice mindfulness, the more you reap rewards.

1. Start by self-monitoring for 1–2 weeks, paying particular attention to specific situations in which you feel strong negative emotions over excessive work demands.

2. Pause and observe each emotion, bringing your attention back to the emotion, rather than any negative thoughts. See if you can "ride" it like a wave, rather than trying to stop it, change it, or push it away.

3. Notice and describe to yourself the physical sensations associated with that emotion. Where in your body do you feel your emotions? Do they change over time as you observe them?

4. Name the emotion ("I am feeling overwhelmed") and then create some mental distance from it as you observe it. Remind yourself that emotions are body signals that you've felt before and will feel again.

5. Accept that you're feeling what you're feeling, and do not try to feel anything else. Find what may be true about your emotion. Consider "thanking" your emotion for trying to help you.

DEAR MAN: Assertive Communication for Work–Life Balance

Leaders often struggle to set and stick to boundaries or advocate for their needs, especially when prioritizing their own wellbeing and life balance. The DEAR MAN skill from DBT (described in detail in chapter 5) can help you achieve greater work–life balance by providing a structured approach to assertively communicate your needs clearly and confidently, ensuring that you maintain healthy boundaries and relationships while fulfilling your professional responsibilities.

For example, if you are asked to take on an additional project at work that threatens to throw off the work–life balance you have been trying to achieve and maintain, you can use DEAR MAN to navigate the conversation with your boss:

1. Describe. State the situation factually ("I've been staying late at work every evening").

2. Express. Share your feelings ("I'm feeling concerned about missing valuable time with my partner and children").

3. Assert. Clearly state your need ("I need to leave work on time at least three days a week").

4. Reinforce. Highlight why they should grant your request ("This will help me feel more balanced and actually improve my focus at work").

5. (Stay) Mindful. Try not to become embroiled in things going on around you (or inside you!). Instead, do your best to stay centered on the conversation and keep it on course. Stay focused on your goal.

6. Appear confident. Try to maintain a calm, confident demeanor, regardless of how you feel on the inside.

7. Negotiate. Remember that you aren't demanding anything, you're asking for something that you deserve. Be willing to alter your request to make it more appealing to your boss and to find a compromise if necessary.

Values Clarification and Committed Action

Values clarification and committed action involve identifying what's truly important in your life and then taking steps to live in accordance with those values, even when facing challenges. By helping you to identify and prioritize what truly matters to you beyond work, values clarification can significantly enhance your ability to achieve a better work–life balance.

Leaders often become so focused on professional responsibilities that they lose sight of their personal values. Values clarification allows you to reflect on what you want your life to stand for and how much time and resources you want to invest in different areas of your life. By actively exploring questions like "What kind of leader do I want to be?" or "What roles do my health and family play in my sense of fulfillment?" you can clarify your core values and commit to aligning your actions with them. This is then achieved by making conscious decisions that prioritize and balance what you value at work and in your personal life in a way that feels both meaningful and sustainable. Doing this, you will learn that you can be successful at work while also nurturing your personal wellbeing, resulting in a more balanced, purpose-driven approach to both career and life.

1. Reflect on your core values. Take some time to think about the various areas of your personal life that are meaningful to you in addition to work. Then, think about what you value most in each of these areas. For example, work may include leadership, creativity, teamwork, and service. And your personal life may include family, friendships, health, and personal growth.

2. Rate the current alignment of your core values. On a scale from 0 to 10 (0 = not at all aligned, 10 = fully aligned), rate how well your current daily actions align with each of your core values. In addition, rate how *balanced* you feel between your work and personal life.

3. Identify misalignments. Review your ratings and consider where you are most out of alignment with your values.

4. Where you have identified areas of misalignment, choose specific actions you can take to realign your daily behaviors with your values. These could be small changes or bigger shifts in how you allocate your time and energy. In particular, if work and personal life are misaligned, what steps can you take to improve the balance? You might think of setting nonnegotiable work hours, scheduling personal time as nonnegotiable, or communicating your boundaries to your team.

5. Commit, reassess, and reflect. After determining the concrete actions you need to take, commit to taking them for a week. At the end of the week, assess how well your actions align with your core values. Reflect on what worked and what could be improved. How did it feel to act in alignment with your values? Where did you face challenges in maintaining work–life balance? What adjustments can you make moving forward?

Defusion

Defusion refers to techniques that are designed to help you create distance between your thoughts and your actions by considering thoughts as mere thoughts rather than as facts. Defusion can foster psychological flexibility, which reduces the influence of negative thinking. In this case, it can help you to achieve better work–life balance by assisting you in creating a psychological distance from the unhelpful thoughts and emotions that fuel overwork and guilt about setting boundaries. For example, leaders often become entangled with thoughts like "If I'm not always available, I'm failing" or "If I'm not working, I'm not productive." Defusion encourages you to practice noticing your thoughts and seeing them merely as mental events, rather than absolute truths.

The same defusion techniques mentioned in previous chapters, such as labeling thoughts ("I'm having the thought that I'm failing my team") or speaking the thought aloud in a silly voice can help reduce the grip that unhelpful work-related thoughts have on you.

Here's a five-step refresher on how to practice defusion, only this time applied to work–life balance, along with a few additional techniques to further enhance it:

1. Spend some time reflecting and identify a recurring unhelpful thought that tends to pull you away from achieving work–life balance. You might come up with "I can't rest until everything is done" or "If I don't stay late, people will think I'm not committed."

2. Name your mind. If your mind were a person or a character, what would it be? Be creative and, ideally, a little humorous. Examples could be "The Taskmaster" or "Captain Responsibility."

3. Externalize your mind's voice. The next time that thought shows up, instead of simply obeying it, respond as if it's coming from your character. You might think, "Ah, there goes The Taskmaster again, telling me to stay late," or "Nice try, Captain Responsibility, but I'm heading home now."

4. Add humor (or irreverence). You might imagine the thought coming from a silly cartoon character, picture the thought wearing a ridiculous outfit, or thank it sarcastically, as in, "Thanks for your input, Taskmaster, but I'm off-duty now."

5. Commit to values-based actions. Anchor yourself in your values by asking yourself, "If I wasn't listening to that thought, what could I be doing right now to create better work–life balance?" Or try "Despite what my mind is telling me, what one small

action could I take right now that aligns more with my value of work–life balance?" This might include leaving the office at a reasonable time, ignoring an after-hours email to spend uninterrupted time with family, or engaging in a self-care activity.

Case Example: Regaining Work–Life Balance as a Senior Executive

Bryan, a 48-year-old senior executive in a large aviation tech company, frequently worked 70-hour weeks, missing family events and personal activities. Despite incredible professional success, Bryan felt increasingly disconnected from his family and personal life. His sleep suffered, his patience dwindled, and he often felt irritable at home. Bryan's internal narrative was dominated by thoughts like "I can't slow down or I'll lose my edge" and "If I spend more time at home, my work will suffer and I'll be replaced." Over time, this led to strained relationships with his wife and two teenaged children.

Bryan began working with an executive coach skilled in CBT. In one session, Bryan identified the recurring unhelpful thought, "If I slow down, all I've worked for will fall apart." Using cognitive restructuring, the executive coach helped Bryan find distortions in the thought and scrutinize its accuracy, ultimately leading Bryan to reframe the thought as "I can delegate effectively without compromising outcomes." Bryan then practiced gradually off-loading tasks to his team and examining the outcome in terms of both his performance and his satisfaction with his work–life balance.

Next, Bryan's executive coach walked him through a values clarification exercise. Bryan realized that family and health were his two top personal values—and that his current behaviors were significantly misaligned with these values. This motivated him to shift his work habits and prioritize his personal commitments. Bryan created a committed action plan, which allowed him to spend more time with his family and also to prioritize exercise.

Using behavioral activation, Bryan committed to scheduling weekly family dinners and at least one weekend outdoor activity a month. He initially felt guilty and restless during these times, but reminded himself of what the executive coach told him: commitment is not just about making a promise or pledge to change but an active engagement in the activities that move you closer to the life that truly matters. Within a few weeks, he noticed that it was easier to commit to these activities, felt his mood improve, and was touched when his children expressed gratitude for his increased presence in their lives.

Bryan was also taught how to use mindfulness when feelings of anxiety or guilt emerged. Instead of avoiding these emotions, he practiced accepting them by naming them and sitting with them, observing them and describing the physical sensations associated with them, and riding them like a wave and allowing them to rise and fall naturally rather than trying to stop them or push them away. Over time, Bryan noticed that it took less and less time for his emotions to pass, and this helped reduce his tendency to engage in impulsive reactions (invariably, overworking) to rid himself of any intense negative feelings.

Finally, Bryan and the executive coach reviewed the DEAR MAN skill and rehearsed how he could communicate his need for work–life balance to his director. When the time came to have the conversation, Bryan found that he could effectively express the impact that overworking was having on his family relationships and ask for more flexible work. He successfully gained support (and respect!) from his director in the process. Using DEAR MAN skills, Bryan learned that he could advocate for his needs clearly and confidently without damaging relationships, which led him to implement the skills more frequently.

After about three months of using CBT with his executive coach, Bryan reported a 40 percent reduction in his work-related stress, as well as improved sleep and stronger family connections. Bryan's leadership effectiveness also increased as he delegated more and modeled work–life balance for his team.

Conclusion

Achieving work–life balance does not mean dividing time equally between work and personal life, but rather ensuring that both domains receive the attention and energy they deserve for you to thrive. Leaders who actively prioritize balance frequently report higher job satisfaction, better mental health, and improved personal and family relationships. However, balancing your work and personal life as a leader is complex, and the shift toward balance requires intentional, persistent effort. As a leader, you must remain vigilant about your core values, set clear boundaries, and make time and space for values-driven activities, knowing you will inevitably slip from time to time. That's okay, as long as you commit to returning to the process. Remember, the goal is not perfection, but balance. As Bryan's case demonstrated, small, persistent changes can lead to profound improvements in work–life balance, setting the stage for long-term success in both personal and professional realms.

Chapter 10

Moving Forward

Now this is not the end. It is not even the beginning of the end. But it is, perhaps, the end of the beginning.

—Winston Churchill

You did it!

By reading this workbook, or even those chapters that relate to your specific mental health challenges and presumably (hopefully!) initiating and persisting with at least a few of the recommended tools, you have now taken the critical first step of regaining control over your mental health and are probably already moving swiftly along the path to becoming the leader you want to be and deserve to be.

We know you are busy and have already devoted much time to this critical first step, so in addition to congratulating you, please allow us to conclude with several thoughts we'd like you to take with you as you move forward without us.

First, we are at a remarkably interesting point in time where several important phenomena are coming together. The first is the recognition among organizational leaders, decision-makers, and academics that leaders' mental health matters. It matters to themselves, to their families, and to their friends, but it also matters to the people who work with them and for them.

Second, the reasons why you behave the way you do as a leader, and how effective you will be as a leader, do not just reside inside the workplace. Instead, there is a growing awareness that many of these influences lie outside of the workplace. As we have seen throughout this book, your mental health and even your family and personal life leave you in a position where you are well-placed for quality leadership—or, unfortunately, where your potential for being the leader you want to be is compromised. The tools we shared throughout this workbook should allow you to not only work on any problems that currently impede your leadership but also dive in and address budding issues before they have a chance to negatively impact your leadership.

Third, the benefits of CBT, DBT, and ACT have been available to us for decades, with ongoing research making refinements and improvements all the time. This book represents the first attempt to apply these evidence-based techniques directly to leaders. It was written by two psychologists: one located in Canada, with decades of experience studying leadership and working with leaders, and the other in the United States, with decades of experience studying evidence-based psychological interventions and implementing them in clinical practice. In other words, we've got you covered!

Fourth, the tools you've explored in this book don't just work at the individual level—they have the power to scale up to your entire organization. One striking example comes from the Norwegian Navy. After the frigate *His Norwegian Majesty's Ship Helge Ingstad* capsized in a catastrophic nighttime collision on November 18, 2018, the entire crew of 137—many of whom were sleeping at the time—survived, but were traumatized. Rather than leaving recovery to individual therapy alone, leadership and practitioners developed a structured, organization-wide application of CBT. Utilizing exposure therapy techniques typically used to treat phobias, the entire crew took part in a 16-day, step-by-step process of returning to sea. Sessions began gradually, starting on solid ground, with open conversations and social support. By days 7 to 9, crew members boarded a similar frigate. At the end of the treatment, all crew members slept aboard overnight. This demonstrates how entire organizations can benefit when CBT is scaled with intention, care, and courageous leadership. Think about what your organization could achieve with that same commitment from you.

Fifth, the challenge now is to consolidate the gains you have made in overcoming any mental health challenges that interfered with your leadership. Sadly, practice does not make perfect (if only!), but persistent practice is the best insurance that any gains you have made will be maintained and that future issues can either be managed more effectively or, ideally, prevented entirely. In the immortal words by Freddie Mercury of the group Queen, "Don't stop me now!"

Finally, think of all these tools as an oxygen mask in an airplane. Before taking off, you are reminded on each and every trip you take that if there is depressurization, you must put your mask on first before assisting a child. Is that because they think you might have forgotten? Or that your child is less important than you? No, it is because you cannot help others if your own health is compromised. In the same way, taking charge of your own mental health is not an act of selfishness. You will not be able to help your employees, your team, your organization, or your family if your own wellbeing is compromised. In this light, looking after yourself is a prosocial act that can benefit so many others—and you deserve it for yourself!

Thank you for joining us, and please, take good care of yourself—and others!

—Julian and Simon

Afterword

I never imagined that I would be a CEO.

And the truth is that most days I'm not quite sure how it happened.

But I did believe that it must be nice to be one, and in many ways that's true.

I have the privilege of working with incredible people doing something that I believe very deeply in.

However, I never fully anticipated the pressures that come with the role.

That heaviness when you feel the responsibility of delivering for both the business and for your colleagues. The inevitable imposter syndrome when things are difficult, wondering if you really are the right person. And the sleepless nights that come from the recurring, unshakable sense of never doing enough, well enough, and of failing both at work and in your personal life.

I have spent a lot of time searching for tools to help me to be able to be at my best both in my professional role and my personal life.

There is a lot of information out there but it is rare to find techniques that really work.

I will admit that I am biased when it comes to Dr. Julian Barling, and that is because long before I ever became a CEO, and in fact well before I was certain of even graduating from university with a passing grade, he changed my life.

In my first year as a university student, he was my professor of organizational behavior. He taught me lessons that I will never forget and that I have held dear ever since: the importance of being vulnerable even in situations where you don't believe you can be, and of empathy in leadership.

As leaders, we have been trained never to show vulnerability for fear of it being interpreted as weakness. And we often find ourselves in situations where empathy is not valued as a leadership trait. What this book teaches us is that if you allow yourself to be vulnerable enough to admit that you need help to manage the self-doubt, stress, anxiety, and difficulty disconnecting, not only will you benefit, but your loved ones will too. There are moments when I feel extremely isolated, that no one understands what I am going through at work and that I can't speak to anyone about it for fear of looking weak. And then my wife will remind me that while she and the kids don't know exactly what is happening day to day, they feel everything that I do through my energy.

It's a powerful reminder that our professional and personal lives are fundamentally intertwined. Whatever we are feeling inside is bound to seep out and impact those around us. As leaders, finding the empathy for ourselves, for our colleagues, and for our families to seek tools that can help us to navigate the day-to-day pressures of leadership is critical for our mental health and to be the best version of ourselves at work and at home.

The challenge is finding tools that really work. In my case, the insights and exercises in this book have proven to be a game changer.

Three areas of this book stood out for me:

- First, the importance of reconnecting with my values and how doing so can help with overcoming mental health challenges such as feelings of burnout as well as with work–life balance and how I show up overall as a leader.

- Second, learning how to identify and replace the unproductive thoughts that arise from self-doubt with constructive perspectives through cognitive restructuring. As leaders we navigate constant uncertainty and pressure, which can lead us to focus on past mistakes and become frozen. With cognitive restructuring, while my stress did not disappear overnight, I became able to reframe challenges and get to potential solutions faster.

- Third, the importance of emotion regulation. In the business world we are often taught that emotions are a liability to be controlled or suppressed. However, this book taught me that emotions—when understood and managed properly—are actually a source of strength. The DBT techniques presented here, especially mindfulness and distress tolerance strategies, can help everyone to navigate high-pressure situations without being overwhelmed with emotions such as stress and fear.

If you are like me, at times you are caught between feeling overwhelmed by the pressures of leadership and feeling like you can't share it with anyone or don't have time to invest in help.

This book provides real tools in a very efficient and effective way that have helped me to better navigate the inherent pressures of leadership while getting more enjoyment from work, hopefully making me a better leader overall and a better husband and father. I highly recommend it as a resource for you and for anyone in leadership positions.

—Tim Coolican
CEO, Milk Makeup, New York

Acknowledgments

Only someone who has written a book can truly appreciate how much is owed to those around them. This book would be incomplete without acknowledging the many individuals who supported, inspired, and challenged us throughout its development. We do so with deep gratitude—and a hint of trepidation—knowing how easy it is to inadvertently overlook someone. Even so, the joy of expressing our thanks far outweighs the risk of omission.

We are both deeply indebted to the exceptional team at New Harbinger Publications. Simon first had the opportunity to pitch this book to Dr. Matthew McKay, founder of New Harbinger, after a chance encounter in the hotel gift shop at the 2022 ADAA conference in Denver, Colorado. We extend our heartfelt thanks to Dr. McKay; Ryan Buresh, acquisitions editor; Madeline Greenhalgh, associate editor; Dr. Jody Gentian Bower, copyeditor; and Amy Shoup, art director. Your guidance, support, and expertise played a vital role in bringing this project to life.

Our collaboration has roots stretching back more than 30 years, to when Simon enrolled in Julian's undergraduate course on experimental and quasi-experimental design at Queen's University in Kingston, Ontario. Though our paths diverged for a time, we reconnected over a decade ago and now count ourselves not just as colleagues, but close friends—a friendship that gives new meaning to the Gallup concept of having a best friend at work.

Much of Simon's inspiration for this book emerged from his experience with the Physician Leadership Program (PLP) at Montefiore Medical Center–Albert Einstein College of Medicine in the Bronx, New York. While the remarkable members of his PLP cohort are too numerous to name individually, their insights profoundly shaped his understanding of leadership. As the first non-physician invited to participate, Simon remains especially grateful to Dr. Jonathan E. Alpert, chair of the Department of Psychiatry and Behavioral Sciences, for his nomination, and to Dr. Jeffrey M. Weiss, senior vice president for medical affairs at Montefiore Einstein and visionary leader of the Physician Leadership Academy, for taking a leap of faith. He would also like to give a special shoutout to the many extraordinary *women* in leadership he has had the privilege to work alongside at Montefiore Einstein—Catherine Skae, MD; Amanda Zayde, PsyD; Sandra Pimentel, PhD; Salimah Velji, MBA, MPH; Sabrina Mueller, LCSW; Michelle Blackmore, PhD; Rachel Held, PhD; Yael Belinkie, PhD; Ana Ozdoba, MD; Shaina Siber-Sanderowitz, LCSW; Laurie Gallo, PhD; Wendy Fuller, PhD, and Shireen Rizvi, PhD—whose intellectual stimulation, insight, and authenticity have been both inspiring and transformative.

Julian's inspiration for this book draws on more than three decades of working with leaders from over 50 companies and teaching in executive development programs and MBA classrooms—both executive and traditional—in Australia, Canada, Chile, Israel, Mexico, Peru, South Africa, and the United States. The perseverance and growth of these leaders—often under immense pressure and with limited resources, time, and training—continue to inspire him and fuel an enduring optimism about what people can achieve when supported and challenged to grow. He is especially grateful to the many women leaders he has worked with—those who, despite navigating organizational cultures not always designed with them in mind, show remarkable commitment to growing their leadership and lifting up others. Alma Hannon first intrigued him about CBT when he was an undergraduate student. Closer to home, Julian offers heartfelt thanks to Lynnette Purda, Gloria Saccon, Kerri Regan, Jana Raver, Olena Ivus, and Katherine Parks, who stepped up when they were needed most. He also honors the achievements of his former PhD students—Sandy Hershcovis, Kara Arnold, Erica Carleton, Colette Hoption, Cindy Suurd Ralph, and Michelle Inness—who have gone on to senior leadership roles in their own universities. Your courage and resilience are a continual inspiration; never underestimate the profound influence you will have on the next generation of leaders in Canada and beyond.

Finally, to our families, friends, colleagues, mentors, and students: thank you for being part of this journey. We carry your influence on every page.

Resources

Introduction

Barling, J. 2014. *The Science of Leadership: Lessons from Research for Organizational Leaders*. New York: Oxford University Press.

Hayes, S. C. 2005. *Get Out of Your Mind and Into Your Life: The New Acceptance and Commitment Therapy*. Oakland, CA: New Harbinger Publications.

McKay, M., Wood, J. C., & Brantley, J. 2019. *The Dialectical Behavior Therapy Skills Workbook: Practical DBT Exercises for Learning Mindfulness, Interpersonal Effectiveness, Emotion Regulation, and Distress Tolerance*. Oakland, CA: New Harbinger Publications.

Rego, S., & Fader, S. 2021. *The CBT Workbook for Mental Health*. New York: Rockridge Press.

Chapter 1

Alberti, R., & Emmons, M. 2017. *Your Perfect Right: Assertiveness and Equality in Your Life and Relationships*. Oakland, CA: New Harbinger Publications.

Chapman, A. L., & Gratz, K. L. 2015. *The Dialectical Behavior Therapy Skills Workbook for Anger: Using DBT Mindfulness and Emotion Regulation Skills to Manage Anger*. Oakland, CA: New Harbinger Publications.

Kabat-Zinn, J. 2024. *Full Catastrophe Living: Using the Wisdom of Your Body and Mind to Face Stress, Pain, and Illness*. 2nd ed. New York: Penguin Random House.

Knaus, W. J. 2021. *The Cognitive Behavioral Workbook for Anger: A Step-by-Step Program for Success*. Oakland, CA: New Harbinger Publications.

Chapter 2

Davis, M., Eshelman, E. R., & McKay, M. 2008. *The Relaxation and Stress Reduction Workbook*. Oakland, CA: New Harbinger Publications.

Leahy, R. L. 2006. *The Worry Cure: Seven Steps to Stop Worry from Stopping You*. Easton, PA: Harmony.

Rego, S. A. 2025. *Panic Disorder and Agoraphobia*. Newburyport, MA: Hogrefe Press.

Robichaud, M., & Buhr, K. 2018. *The Worry Workbook: CBT Skills to Overcome Worry and Anxiety by Facing the Fear of Uncertainty*. Oakland, CA: New Harbinger Publications.

Szuplat, T. 2024. *Say It Well. Find Your Voice, Speak Your Mind, Inspire Any Audience*. New York: Harper Collins.

Chapter 3

Addis, M. E., & Martell, C. R. 2004. *Overcoming Depression One Step at a Time: The New Behavioral Activation Approach to Getting Your Life Back*. Oakland, CA: New Harbinger Publications.

Owen, D. 2008. *In Sickness and in Power: Illness in Heads of Government During the Last 100 Years*. New York: Methuen.

Rego, S., & Fader, S. 2018. *The 10-Step Depression Relief Workbook: A Cognitive Behavioral Therapy Approach*. Berkeley, CA: Callisto Media.

Strosahl, K. D., & Robinson, P. J. 2017. *The Mindfulness and Acceptance Workbook for Depression: Using Acceptance and Commitment Therapy to Move Through Depression and Create a Life Worth Living*. Oakland, CA: New Harbinger Publications.

Chapter 4

HBR Guide to Beating Burnout. 2020. Cambridge, MA: Harvard Business School Press.

Martin, S. 2021. *The Better Boundaries Workbook: A CBT-Based Program to Help You Set Limits, Express Your Needs, and Create Healthy Relationships*. Oakland, CA: New Harbinger Publications.

Maslach, C., & Leiter, M. P. 2022. *The Burnout Challenge: Managing People's Relationships with Their Jobs*. Cambridge, MA: Harvard University Press.

Sorensen, D. 2024. *ACT for Burnout: Recharge, Reconnect, and Transform Burnout with Acceptance and Commitment Therapy*. London: Jessica Kingsley Publishers.

Chapter 5

Gottman, J., & Silver, N. 2015. *The Seven Principles for Making Marriage Work: A Practical Guide from the Country's Foremost Relationship Expert.* Easton, PA: Harmony Books.

Herbert, A., & Pavel, M. P. 2024. *Random Kindness and Senseless Acts of Beauty.* New York: New York University Press.

Chapter 6

Barling, J., Barnes, C. M., Carleton, E., & Wagner, D. T., eds. 2016. *Sleep and Work: Research Insights for the Workplace.* New York: Oxford University Press.

Davidson, J. 2012. *Sink Into Sleep: A Step-by-Step Guide for Reversing Insomnia.* New York: Demos Health.

Huffington, A. 2017. *The Sleep Revolution: Transforming Your Life, One Night at a Time.* Easton, PA: Harmony Books.

Silberman, S. 2009. *The Insomnia Workbook: A Comprehensive Guide to Getting the Sleep You Need.* Oakland, CA: New Harbinger Publications.

Chapter 7

DuFrene, T., & Wilson, K. 2012. *The Wisdom to Know the Difference: An Acceptance and Commitment Therapy Workbook for Overcoming Substance Abuse.* Oakland, CA: New Harbinger Publications.

Frone, M. R. 2013. *Alcohol and Illicit Drug Use in the Workforce and Workplace.* Washington, DC: American Psychological Association.

Glasner-Edwards, S. 2015. *The Addiction Recovery Skills Workbook: Changing Addictive Behaviors Using CBT, Mindfulness, and Motivational Interviewing Techniques.* Oakland, CA: New Harbinger Publications.

Williams, R. E., & Kraft, J. S. 2012. *The Mindfulness Workbook for Addiction: A Guide to Coping with the Grief, Stress, and Anger That Trigger Addictive Behaviors.* Oakland, CA: New Harbinger Publications.

Chapter 8

Clarke, M. 2024. *Never Not Working: Why the Always-On Culture Is Bad for Business—and How to Fix It*. Boston: Harvard Business School Press.

Martin, S. 2019. *The CBT Workbook for Perfectionism: Evidence-Based Skills to Help You Let Go of Self-Criticism, Build Self-Esteem, and Find Balance*. Oakland, CA: New Harbinger Publications.

Robinson, B. E. 2014. *Chained to the Desk: A Guidebook for Workaholics, Their Partners and Children, and the Clinicians Who Treat Them*. New York: New York University Press.

Chapter 9

Kelly, M. 2011. *Off Balance: Getting Beyond the Work–Life Balance Myth to Personal and Professional Satisfaction*. New York: Penguin.

Tawwab, N. G. 2021. *Set Boundaries, Find Peace: A Guide to Reclaiming Yourself*. New York: Penguin Random House.

Endnotes

1   Marrs, R. W. 1995. "A Meta-Analysis of Bibliotherapy Studies." *American Journal of Community Psychology*, 23: 843–869.

2   Gregory, R. J., et al. 2004. "Cognitive Bibliotherapy for Depression: A Meta-Analysis." *Professional Psychology: Research and Practice*, 35(3): 275–280.

3   Scogin, F., et al. 1989. "Comparative Efficacy of Cognitive and Behavioral Bibliotherapy for Mildly and Moderately Depressed Older Adults." *Journal of Consulting and Clinical Psychology*, 57(3): 403–407.

4   Beaty, D., & Barling, J. 1982. *Positive Exam Results—Without Stress*. Johannesburg:: McGraw-Hill.

5   Jones-Rincon, A., & Howard, K. J. 2019. "Anxiety in the Workplace: A Comprehensive Occupational Health Evaluation of Anxiety Disorders in Public School Teachers." *Journal of Applied Biobehavioral Research*, 24: e12133.

6   Villarroel, M. A., & Terlizzi, E. P. 2020. "Symptoms of Depression Among Adults: United States, 2019." *NCHS Data Brief*, No. 379.

7   Keller, T. 1999. "Images of the Familiar: Individual Differences and Implicit Leadership Theories." *Leadership Quarterly*, 10: 589–607.

8   Epitropaki, O., & Martin, R. 2005. "From Ideal to Real: A Longitudinal Study of the Role of Implicit Leadership Theories on Leader-Member Exchanges and Employee Outcomes." *Journal of Applied Psychology*, 90(4): 659–676.

9   Cloutier, A., & Barling, J. 2023. "Expectations of Leaders' Mental Health." *Leadership and Organization Developmental Journal*, 30: 276–296.

10   Cain, Á. 2017. "11 Successful People Who Get By on Hardly Any Sleep." *Business Insider*.

11   Cain, Á. "11 Successful People."

12   Lin, J., et al. 2019. "The Dark Side of Transformational Leader Behaviors for Leaders Themselves: A Conservation of Resources Perspective." *Academy of Management Journal*, 62: 1556–1582.

13   Deloitte & LifeWorks Research Group. 2021. "Inspiring Insights: Well-Being and Resilience in Senior Leaders."

14   Reynolds, E. 2024. "Stressed to Impress." The British Psychological Society.

15   Barling, J. 2014. *The Science of Leadership: Lessons from Research for Organizational Leaders*. New York: Oxford University Press.

16   Zwingmann, I., et al. 2016. "Every Light Has Its Shadow: A Longitudinal Study of Transformational Leadership and Leaders' Emotional Exhaustion." *Journal of Applied Social Psychology*, 46: 19–33.

17   Lin, "The Dark Side of Transformational Leader Behaviors for Leaders Themselves."

18   Li, F., et al. 2023. "Serving While Being Energized (Strained)? A Dual-Path Model Linking Servant Leadership to Leader Psychological Strain and Job Performance." *Journal of Applied Psychology*, 108(4): 660–675.

19   Rundle, A. G., et al. 2018. "Business Travel and Behavioral and Mental Health." *Journal of Occupational and Environmental Medicine*, 60(7): 612–616.

20 Richards, C. A. & Rundle, A. G. 2011. "Business Travel and Self-Rated Health, Obesity, and Cardiovascular Disease Risk Factors." *Journal of Occupational and Environmental Medicine,* 53(4): 358–363.

21 Cook, S. C., et al. 2017. "Evidence-Based Psychotherapy: Advantages and Challenges." *Neurotherapeutics,* 14: 537-545.

22 Larocca, A. 2025. *How to Be Well: Navigating Our Self-Care Epidemic, One Dubious Cure At a Time.* New York: Knopf.

23 David, D., et al. 2018. "Why Cognitive Behavioral Therapy Is the Current Gold Standard of Psychotherapy." *Frontiers in Psychiatry,* 9: 333730.

24 Fordham, B., et al. 2021. "The Evidence for Cognitive Behavioral Therapy in Any Condition, Population, or Context: A Meta-Review of Systematic Reviews and Panoramic Meta-Analysis." *Psychological Medicine,* 51: 21–29.

25 Linehan, M. M. 1993. *Cognitive-Behavioral Treatment of Borderline Personality Disorder.* New York: Guilford Press.

26 Rizvi, S. L., et al. 2024. "The State of the Science: Dialectical Behavior Therapy." *Behavior Therapy,* 55: 1232–1248.

27 Hayes, S. C., et al. 1999. *Acceptance and Commitment Therapy: An Experiential Approach to Behavior Change.* New York: Guilford Press.

28 Gloster, A. T., et al. 2020. "The Empirical Status of Acceptance and Commitment Therapy: A Review of Meta-Analyses." *Journal of Contextual Behavioral Science,* 18: 181–192.

29 van Agteren, J., et al. 2021. "A Systematic Review and Meta-Analysis of Psychological Interventions to Improve Mental Wellbeing." *Nature Human Behaviour,* 5(5): 631–652.

30 Goetzel, R. Z., et al. 2002. "The Business Case for Quality Mental Health Services: Why Employers Should Care About the Mental Health and Well-Being of Their Employees." *Journal of Occupational and Environmental Medicine,* 44(4): 320–330

31 Kazdin, A. E. 2024. "Interventions in Everyday Life to Improve Mental Health and Reduce Symptoms of Psychiatric Disorders." *American Psychologist,* 79: 185–209.

32 Shao, B. 2024. "The Leader Affect Revolution Reloaded: Toward an Integrative Framework and Robust Science." *Journal of Organizational Behavior,* 35: 101754.

33 Schwartzmüller, T., et al. 2018. "Sparking Anger and Anxiety: Why Intense Leader Anger Displays Trigger Both More Deviance and Higher Work Effort in Followers." *Journal of Business and Psychology,* 33: 761–777.

34 Porat, R., & Paluck, E. L. 2024. "Anger at Work." *Frontiers in Social Psychology,* 2: 1–19.

35 Schwartmüller, "Sparking Anger and Anxiety."

36 Shao, "The Leader Affect Revolution Reloaded."

37 Wang, L., et al. 2018. "Does Anger Expression Help or Harm Leader Effectiveness? The Role of Competence-Based Versus Integrity-Based Violations and Abusive Supervision." *Academy of Management Journal,* 61: 1050–1072.

38 Ames, D. R., & Flynn, F. J. 2007. "What Breaks a Leader: The Curvilinear Relation Between Assertiveness and Leadership." *Journal of Personality and Social Psychology,* 92: 307–324; and Staw, B. M., et al. 2019. "Leadership in the Locker Room: How the Intensity of Leaders' Unpleasant Affective Displays Shapes Team Performance." *Journal of Applied Psychology,* 104: 1547–1557.

39 Beck, R., & Fernandez, E. 1998. "Cognitive-Behavioral Therapy in the Treatment of Anger: A Meta-Analysis." *Cognitive Therapy and Research,* 22: 63–74.

40 O'Reilly, J., et al. 2015. "Is Negative Attention Better Than No Attention? The Comparative Effects of Ostracism and Harassment At Work." *Organization Science,* 26: 774–793.

41 Kessler, R. C., et al. 2006. "The Epidemiology of Panic Attacks, Panic Disorder, and Agoraphobia in the National Comorbidity Survey Replication." *Archives of General Psychiatry,* 63(4): 415–424.

42 Jones-Rincon, A., & Howard, K. J. 2019. "Anxiety in the Workplace: A Comprehensive Occupational Health Evaluation of Anxiety Disorders in Public School Teachers." *Journal of Applied Biobehavioral Research,* 24: e12133.

43 Walsh, M. M., et al. 2024. "Leader Mindfulness, Passive Leadership, and the Mediating Role of Leader Anxiety." *Journal of Personnel Psychology*, 23(4): 213–219.

44 Barling, *The Science of Leadership*.

45 Byrne, A., et al. 2014. "The Depleted Leader: The Influence of Leaders' Diminished Psychological Resources on Leadership Behaviors." *Leadership Quarterly*, 25: 344–357.

46 Mawritz, M. B., et al. 2013. "Supervisors Exceedingly Difficult Goals and Abusive Supervision: The Mediating Effects of Hindrance Stress, Anger, and Anxiety." *Journal of Organizational Behavior*, 35: 358–372.

47 Xi, M., et al. 2020. "Feeling Anxious and Low Performers: A Multilevel Model of High-Performance Work Systems and Abusive Supervision." *Journal of Organizational Behavior*, 43: 91–111.

48 Szuplat, T. 2024. *Say It Well. Find Your Voice, Speak Your Mind, Inspire Any Audience*. New York: Harper Collins.

49 Ghaemi, N. 2011. *A First-Rate Madness: Uncovering the Links Between Leadership and Mental Illness*. New York: Penguin Books.

50 Kellett, J. B., et al. 2006. "Empathy and the Emergence of Task and Relations Leaders." *Leadership Quarterly*, 17: 146–162.

51 Byrne, "The Depleted Leader."

52 Gorman, J. M. 1996. "Comorbid Depression and Anxiety Spectrum Disorders." *Depression and Anxiety*, 4: 160–168.

53 Lai, H. M. X. 2015. "Prevalence of Comorbid Substance Use, Anxiety and Mood Disorders in Epidemiological Surveys, 1990–2014: A Systematic Review and Meta-Analysis." *Drug and Alcohol Dependence*, 154: 1–13.

54 NCHS. 2021. "Latest Pulse Survey on Anxiety and Depression During Pandemic." NCHS: A Blog of the National Center for Health Statistics.

55 Barling, *The Science of Leadership*.

56 UW Foster School of Business. 2022. "Foster Insights—Ryan Fehr." YouTube video.

57 WHO. 2019. "Burn-Out an 'Occupational Phenomenon': International Classification of Diseases." World Health Organization.

58 Maslach, C., & Jackson, S. E. 1981. "The Measurement of Experienced Burnout." *Journal of Occupational Behavior*, 2: 99-113.

59 Clarke, M. 2024. *Never Not Working: Why the Always-On Culture Is Bad for Business—and How to Fix It*. Boston: Harvard Business School Press.

60 Dicke, T., et al. 2022. "Ubiquitous Emotional Exhaustion in School Principals: Stable Trait, Enduring Autoregressive Trend, or Occasion-Specific State?" *Journal of Educational Psychology*, 114(2): 426–441.

61 Lacerenza, C. N., et al. 2017. "Leadership Training Design, Delivery, and Implementation: A Meta-Analysis." *Journal of Applied Psychology*, 102: 1686–1718.

62 Lyall, S. 2024. "We Have All Hit a Wall." *New York Times*.

63 Dicke, "Ubiquitous Emotional Exhaustion in School Principals."

64 Olson, K., et al. 2019. "Cross-Sectional Survey of Workplace Stressors Associated with Physician Burnout Measured by the Mini-Z and Maslach Burnout Inventory." *Stress and Health*, 35: 157–175.

65 Spencer-Hwang, R., et al. 2024. "Prevalence of Burnout Among Public Health Professionals: A Systematic Review." *Journal of Public Health Management and Practice*, 30: 384–392.

66 Courtright S. H., et al. 2014. "Fired Up or Burned Out? How Developmental Challenge Differentially Impacts Leader Behavior." *Journal of Applied Psychology*, 99: 681–696.

67 Barling, J., & Frone, M. R. 2017. "If Only My Leader Would Just Do *Something*! Passive Leadership Undermines Employee Wellbeing Through Role Stressors and Psychological Resource Depletion." *Stress and Health*, 33: 211–222.

68 Bandura, A. 1997. *Self-Efficacy: The Exercise of Self-Control*. New York: W. H. Freeman and Company.

69   Ouweneel, E., et al. 2013 "Do-It-Yourself: An Online Positive Psychology Intervention to Promote Positive Emotions, Self-Efficacy, and Engagement at Work." *Career Development International,* 18: 173–195.

70   Røsand, G-M., et al. 2013. "Relationship Dissatisfaction and Other Risk Factors for Future Relationship Dissolution: A Population-Based Study of 18,523 Couples." *Social Psychiatry and Psychiatric Epidemiology,* 28: 109–119.

71   Johnson, N. J., et al. 2000. "Marital Status and Mortality: The National Longitudinal Mortality Study." *Annals of Epidemiology,* 10(4): 224–238.

72   Prouix, C. M., et al. 2007. "Marital Quality and Personal Wellbeing: A Meta-Analysis." *Journal of Marriage and the Family,* 69: 576–593.

73   Be, D., et al. 2013. "Prospective Associations Between Marital Adjustment and Life Satisfaction." *Personal Relationships,* 20: 728–739.

74   Whisman, M. A., et al. 2018. "Marital Satisfaction and Mortality in the United States Adult Population." *Health Psychology,* 37(11): 1041–1044.

75   Dionisi, A., & Barling, J. 2019. "What Happens at Home Doesn't Stay at Home: The Role of Family and Romantic Partner Conflict in Destructive Leadership." *Stress and Health,* 35: 304–317.

76   Cho, C., et al. 2023. "Do Married CEOs Foster More Efficient Innovation?" *Review of Financial Economics,* 41: 242–268.

77   Fong, M.-L., & Tower, T. 2023. "How CEO Divorce Impacts Firm Performance." *Concordia University News*.

78   Dumas, T. L., & Stanko, T. L. 2017. "Married with Children: How Family Role Identification Shapes Leadership Behaviors at Work." *Personnel Psychology,* 70: 598–633.

79   Dionisi & Barling, "What Happens at Home."

80   Baumeister, R. F., et al. 2001. "Bad Is Stronger Than Good." *Review of General Psychology,* 5(4): 323–370.

81   Lin, S.-H., et al. 2021. "Positive Family Events Facilitate Effective Leader Behaviors at Work: A Within-Individual Investigation of Family-Work Enrichment." *Journal of Applied Psychology,* 106: 1412–1434.

82   Leavitt, K., et al. 2019. "From the Bedroom to the Office: Workplace Spillover Effects of Sexual Activity at Home." *Journal of Management,* 45: 1173–1192.

83   Joseph, D. L., et al. 2015. "Is a Happy Leader a Good Leader? A Meta-Analytic Investigation of Leader Trait Affect and Leadership." *Leadership Quarterly,* 26: 557–576.

84   Freeman, H., Simons, J., & Benson, N. F. 2023. Romantic Duration, Relationship Quality, and Attachment Insecurity Among Dating Couples. *International Journal of Environmental Research and Public Health*, 20(1), 856.

85   Duncan, R. D., 2018. "Close Encounters: Leadership and Handwritten Notes." *Forbes*.

86   Baumeister, "Bad Is Stronger Than Good."

87   Gottman, J., & Silver, N. 2015. *The Seven Principles for Making Marriage Work: A Practical Guide from the Country's Foremost Relationship Expert*. New York: Harmony.

88   Knutson, K. L., et al. 2010. "Trends in the Prevalence of Short Sleepers in the USA: 1975–2006." *Sleep,* 33(1): 37.

89   Luckhaupt, S. E., et al. 2010. "The Prevalence of Short Sleep Duration by Industry and Occupation in the National Health Interview Study." *Sleep*, 33: 149–159.

90   Kessler, R. C., et al. 2011. "Insomnia and the Performance of US Workers: Results from the America Insomnia Survey." *Sleep,* 34: 1161–1171.

91   Barnes, C. M., et al. 2015. "'You Wouldn't Like Me When I Am Sleepy': Leaders' Sleep, Daily Abusive Supervision, and Work Unit Engagement." *Academy of Management Journal,* 58: 1419–1437.

92   Tepper, B. 2000. "Consequence of Abusive Supervision." *Academy of Management Journal,* 43: 178–190.

93   Barnes, C. M., et al. 2017. "Helping Employees Sleep Well: Effects of Cognitive Behavioral Therapy for Insomnia on Work Outcomes." *Journal of Applied Psychology,* 102: 104–113.

94   Olsen, O. K., et al. 2016. "The Effects of Sleep Deprivation on Leadership Behavior in Military Officers: An Experimental Study." *Journal of Sleep Research,* 25: 683–685.

95   Barnes, "You Wouldn't Like Me When I Am Sleepy."

96   Bootzin, R. R. 1975. "A Stimulus Control Treatment for Insomnia." *Proceedings of the American Psychological Association*, 395–396.

97   Trauer, J. M., et al. 2015. "Cognitive Behavioral Therapy for Insomnia: A Systematic Review and Meta-Analysis." *Archives of Internal Medicine,* 163(3): 191–205.

98   Muench, A., et al. 2022. "We Know CBT-I Works, Now What?" *Faculty Reviews*, 11: 4.

99   Yuan, Z., et al. 2018. "Bad Behavior Keeps You Up at Night: Counterproductive Work Behaviors and Insomnia." *Journal of Applied Psychology,* 103: 383–398.

100   Frone, M. R. 2013. *Alcohol and Illicit Drug Use in the Workforce and Workplace.* Washington, DC: American Psychological Association.

101   Frone, M. R. 2003. "Predictors of Overall and on-the-Job Substance Use Among Young Workers." *Journal of Occupational Health Psychology,* 8(1): 39–54.

102   Frone, M. R. 2006a. "Prevalence and Distribution of Illicit Drug Use in the Workforce and in the Workplace: Findings and Implications from a U.S. National Survey." *Journal of Applied Psychology,* 91: 856–869.

103   Frone, M. R. 2006b. Prevalence and Distribution of Alcohol Use and Impairment in the Workplace: A U.S. National Survey. *Journal of Studies on Alcohol,* 67(1): 147–156.

104   Frone, "Prevalence and Distribution of Illicit Drug Use"; Frone, "Prevalence and Distribution of Alcohol Use and Impairment."

105   Frone, *Alcohol and Illicit Drug Use in the Workforce and Workplace.*

106   Ayalla-Somayajula, D., et al. 2025. "Trends in Alcohol Use After the COVID-19 Pandemic: A National Cross-Sectional Study." *Annals of Internal Medicine,* 178: 138–140.

107   Greenwood, J., et al. 2022. "Substance Use During the Pandemic: Implications for Labor Force Participation." NBER Working Paper, 29912.

108   Streufert, S., et al. 1994. "Alcohol and Managerial Performance." *Journal of Studies on Alcohol and Drugs,* 55: 230–238.

109   Streufert, S., et al. 1995. "Alcohol Hangover and Managerial Effectiveness." *Alcoholism: Clinical and Experimental Research,* 19: 1141–1146.

110   Streufert, S. 1997. "Excess Coffee Consumption in Simulated Complex Work Settings: Detriment or Facilitation of Performance?" *Journal of Applied Psychology,* 82: 774–782.

111   Byrne, "The Depleted Leader."

112   Quoted in Norville, D. 1971. *Back on Track: How to Straighten Out Your Life When It Throws You a Curve.* New York: Simon & Schuster, 201.

113   Oates, W. 1972. *Confessions of a Workaholic: The Facts About Work Addiction.* New York: World Publishing.

114   Clarke, M., et al. 2016. "All Work and No Play? A Meta-Analytic Examination of the Correlates and Outcomes of Workaholism." *Journal of Management,* 42: 1836–1873.

115   Tarris, T. W., & de Jonge, J. 2024. "Workaholism: Taking Stock and Looking Forward." *Annual Review of Organizational Psychology and Organizational Behavior,* 11: 113–138.

116   Andersen, F. B., et al. 2023. "The Prevalence of Workaholism: A Systematic Review and Meta-Analysis." *Frontiers in Psychology,* 14: 1252372.

117   Alessandri, G., et al. 2020. "The Costs of Working Too Hard: Relationships Between Workaholism, Job Demands, and Prosocial Organizational Citizenship Behavior." *Journal of Personnel Psychology,* 19(1): 24–32.

118   Clarke, "All Work and No Play?"

119   Menghini, L., & Balducci, C. 2024. "The Daily Costs of Workaholism: A Within-Individual Investigation on Blood Pressure, Emotional Exhaustion, and Sleep Disturbances." *Journal of Occupational Health Psychology,* 29: 201–219.

120   Dong, Y., & Li, W. 2024. "Leader Workaholism and Subordinates' Psychological Distress: The Moderating Role of Justice Climate." *Acta Psychologica,* 246: 104288.

121   Bakker, A. B., et al. 2009. "Workaholism and Relationship Quality: A Spillover-Crossover Perspective." *Journal of Occupational Health Psychology,* 14: 23–33.

122   Clarke, "All Work and No Play?"

123   Xu, X., et al. 2023. "Does Working Hard Really Pay Off? Testing the Temporal Ordering Between Workaholism and Job Performance." *Journal of Organizational and Occupational Psychology,* 96: 503–523.

124   Clarke, *Never Not Working.*

125   Alessandri, "The Costs of Working Too Hard."

126   Balducci, C., et al. 2012. "Exploring the Relationship Between Workaholism and Workplace Aggressive Behavior: The Role of Job-Related Emotion." *Personality and Individual Differences,* 53: 629–634.

127   Mackey, J. D., et al. 2017. "Abusive Supervision: A Meta-Analysis and Empirical Review." *Journal of Management,* 43: 1940–1965.

128   Dasborough, M. T., et al. 2009. "What Goes Around Comes Around: How Meso-Level Negative Emotional Contagion Can Ultimately Determine Organizational Attitudes Toward Leaders." *Leadership Quarterly,* 20: 571–585.

129   Rodell, J. B. 2024. "'I'm So Stressed!': The Relational Consequences of Stress Bragging." *Personnel Psychology,* 77: 1441–1465.

130   Doll, J. 2012. "When Men Give Women Career Advice." *The Atlantic.*

131   Frone, M. R. 2000. "Work–Family Conflict and Employee Psychiatric Disorders: The National Comorbidity Survey." *Journal of Applied Psychology,* 85(6): 888–895.

132   Vahedi, A., et al. 2019. "Crossover of Parents' Work-Family Conflict to Family Functioning and Child Mental Health." *Journal of Applied Developmental Psychology,* 62(3): 38–49.

133   Dionisi & Barling, "What Happens at Home."

134   McClean, S. T., et al. 2021. "Transformed by the Family: An Attachment Theory Perspective on Family Work-Enrichment and Transformational Leadership." *Journal of Applied Psychology,* 106: 1848–1866.

135   McClean, "Transformed by the Family," 1853.

136   McClean, "Transformed by the Family," 1856.

137   Lin, "Positive Family Events Facilitate Effective Leader Behaviors at Work."

Julian Barling, PhD, is the Distinguished University Professor, and Borden chair of leadership at the Smith School of Business at Queen's University in Kingston, ON, Canada. He is a fellow of the Royal Society of Canada, the Association of Psychological Science, the Society for Industrial and Organizational Psychology, the European Association for Occupational Health Psychological Association, and the Canadian Psychological Association. He received the Outstanding Career Contribution in Occupational Health Psychology from the European Association for Occupational Health Psychology in 2008; the Distinguished Scientific Contribution from the Canadian Society for Industrial and Organizational Psychology in 2016; and the Lifetime Career Achievement in Research Award from the American Psychological Association, NIOSH, and the Society for Occupational Health Psychology in 2017. He was listed in the top 2 percent of the world's most cited scientists in 2020 and 2022.

Simon Rego, PsyD, is chief of psychology at Montefiore Medical Center and professor of psychiatry and behavioral sciences at Albert Einstein College of Medicine in New York, NY. He is board certified in cognitive behavioral psychology by the American Board of Professional Psychology, certified in cognitive behavior therapy by the Canadian Association of Cognitive and Behavioral Therapies, and certified as a trainer/consultant by the Academy of Cognitive and Behavioral Therapies. He is a fellow of the American Psychological Association (Division 12), the Association for Behavioral and Cognitive Therapies, and the Academy of Cognitive and Behavioral Therapies, and a founding clinical fellow of the Anxiety and Depression Association of America.

Foreword writer **Judith S. Beck, PhD**, is president of the Beck Institute for Cognitive Behavior Therapy, and clinical professor of psychology in psychiatry at the University of Pennsylvania. She is author of the seminal text, *Cognitive Therapy*, which has been translated into more than twenty languages.

Afterword writer **Tim Coolican** "stumbled into" the cosmetics industry, working on Unilever's DermaSilk hair-care brand as an intern. After graduating, he held several roles at Unilever before joining L'Oréal Canada in 2004. Coolican was named president of L'Oréal Paris USA in 2017. He is currently CEO of Milk Makeup, a New York City-based cosmetics and skin-care company.

MORE BOOKS from
NEW HARBINGER PUBLICATIONS

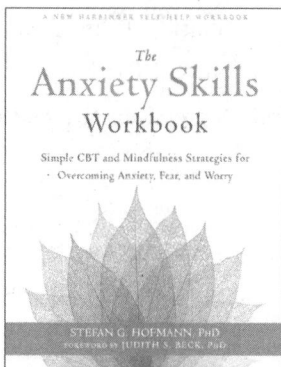

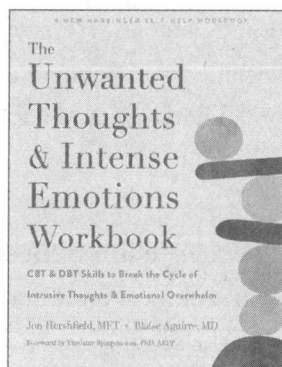